W9-BRE-509

COLORADO

A Photographic Journey

TEXT: **Bill Harris**

CAPTIONS: **Fleur Robertson**

DESIGNED BY: **Teddy Hartshorn**

EDITORIAL: **Gill Waugh and Fleur Robertson**

PRODUCTION: **Ruth Arthur and David Proffit**

DIRECTOR OF PRODUCTION: **Gerald Hughes**

DIRECTOR OF PUBLISHING: **David Gibbon**

CLB 2456
© 1990 Colour Library Books Ltd., Godalming, Surrey, England.
All rights reserved.
This 1990 edition published by Crescent Books,
distributed by Outlet Book Company, Inc., a Random House Company,
225 Park Avenue South, New York, New York 10003.
Printed and bound in Hong Kong.
ISBN 0 517 01493 9
h g f e d c b a

COLORADO

A Photographic Journey

Text by
BILL HARRIS

CRESCENT BOOKS
NEW YORK

The first Europeans found their way to the Rocky Mountains chasing a dream. It was a dream, that is, if you can consider greed and lust a proper inspiration for such things. And in this case the dream was inspired by a pack of lies.

Those first explorers were Spanish. They had long since colonized Mexico and were looking for new riches and adventure. They had brought the Word of God and "civilization," not to mention horses, to the Indians of the southwest. They had introduced them to slavery, with the natives filling the role of slaves, and they had infected them with diseases the red man never knew existed.

By the time they had begun to move north and establish a number of settlements along the Rio Grande down in Texas, word had spread among the Indians that it wasn't all that wonderful to have these people as neighbors. There were two ways to get rid of them. One was to fight, which their brothers to the south had found was a foolish idea, the other was to give them what they seemed to want: new worlds to conquer, preferably rich worlds.

And so the stories began. There are seven great cities to the north, they said. And mountains filled with gold and silver. "Why stay here where all we have are poor farms?" asked the Indians, "when there is so much of what you're looking for just a few day's journey away?" "Why, indeed," replied the Spaniards. And in 1540, Francisco Vasquez de Coronado, with an entourage of four hundred smartly outfitted conquistadores, a thousand Indians to take care of them, another thousand horses and mules to carry their gear, herds of goats and sheep to feed them and a procession of priests and monks to make it all seem legitimate, began marching in search of the fabulous Seven Cities of Cibolla.

There are historians who say Coronado never actually set foot in Colorado. Others contend that he saw the Royal Gorge. But the story that's the most fun to believe is that the procession crossed paths with a lone Indian who volunteered to show them the way to one of the cities, which he called Quivera, where they would find streets paved with gold and marble houses with precious stones used for windows. For some reason, the Spaniards trusted this particular Indian. Maybe it was because they liked his looks. He looked so much like a Turk they called him El Turko. Most likely they believed him because they had been trekking over rough terrain for more than a year and hadn't found so much as a zircon.

Whatever the reason, El Turko became Coronado's right-hand man and the hand was pointed north. As they passed from village to village, the Indians, possibly responding to an El Turko wink, would always say, "Oh, yes! You're almost there. Keep on trekking." Somehow, none of those conquistadores, none of those priests, none of those monks, even the great Coronado himself, ever asked: "How come if all those riches are just over the next hill you people aren't living any better than this?"

A dream can do that to a man.

El Turko led the parade out to the Great Plains and still they kept going north and east. Finally, after long weeks in the hot sun, it dawned on Coronado that he just might be in the company of a liar. With very little ceremony, he strangled the Indian.

But what if El Turko hadn't been a liar? Coronado couldn't help wondering about that. He set up a winter camp and began making plans to continue his search in the spring.

Meanwhile, one of the time-killing entertainments in the winter camp was horse racing and Coronado was an avid participant. It isn't known whether there were any two-peso bets riding with him, but one of his races ended abruptly when the leader fell from his horse and was trampled by another. The thought of recovering out there in the middle of Kansas dimmed the dream considerably and he ordered his men to strike camp and head back to the southwest. He never returned.

The Coronado expedition went home no richer than when it had started. But the Spanish court was convinced that they had just made a wrong turn somewhere and that there were incredible riches in those mountains.

One of the favorites of the court was a man named Hernande Soto, who had gone to Peru some years before and had taken treasure away from another Spaniard, Francisco Pizzaro, who had gotten it in the first place by conquering the Incas. De Soto was anxious to flnd treasure of his own and got permission to finance an expedition more than twice the size of Coronado's.

His route took him up the Mississippi River, where his troops had a high old time killing Indians, raping their women and burning their villages. He also wound up in Kansas. While he was there he came down with a fever and died. His troops marched on without him and, in 1542, finally made it to the mountains of Colorado. They spent the summer looking for the gold, but when the winter winds started to blow they lost their enthusiasm and, like Coronado, headed for home.

Dreams die hard, though, and for another 250 years, Spanish explorers came and went. Some of them found gold, others found silver. The Indians may have exaggerated, but they weren't lying when they said there were riches in the Rockies.

The French were exploring the Rockies by the early part of the eighteenth century, but unlike the Spanish, who lusted after glory as much as gold and therefore talked a lot, the French believed that the fewer people who knew you were getting rich, the fewer would want to share the wealth. They quietly went about their business, usually alone, and many did get rich by hunting and trapping.

There have always been riches for the taking in the Rocky Mountains. But for many, the real riches are the mountains themselves.

The Rocky Mountains are easily the most scenic place in the world, with a naturally rugged and pristine quality that gives different inspiration to different people. The mountains inspire the imagination with vistas of indescribable grandeur in many places, and vistas of complete tranquility in others. Nothing is quite as soul-soothing as listening to the breeze in the trees while you're looking at a peaceful mountain lake in the early evening quiet. No matter where your eye takes you: up at prodigious peaks that are thick with snow-dusted pines in winter; out over wheat fields at midday when light and shadows create a landscape that can only be described as surreal; or through the newly constructed labyrinth of skyscrapers that compete for attention with the mountains on the horizon in Denver, one of the fastest-growing cities in America, you know that these places, these mountains, are very special places indeed.

The mountains themselves have been here for millions of years and seem determined to remain for millions more, in spite of the fact that man has tried over and over again to conquer and tame them. No matter what man does, though, he usually ends up coming to terms with their uncompromising force. All who try to change the landscape find out sooner or later that it's best to succumb to its authoritative voice and learn to be obedient to its dominance.

The voice of the mountains is subtle and often undecipherable, but then it is a voice that one must listen to very carefully. The sound of the wind in the trees can be a signal to a climber that a thunderstorm is coming and a climber who listens well will live to climb again. But people who resist the message will find that tragedy can occur unexpectedly. The mountains will go on living no matter what they do!

The very first explorers found the mountains a barrier. Only the hardiest tried to go through them or over them, and it wasn't until the 1850s that the lure of gold made the Rockies a destination for people on the move. Today, of course, Colorado and the Rockies are destinations for travelers from all over the world. Magnificent scenery is one reason. Water is another. The sun is perhaps the most important of all.

The mountains give you a feeling of completion and a sense of renewal both at the same time. They create delight as well as opportunity, a religious reverence as well as a feeling of freedom from the problems of everyday life. A visitor who can feel a process of interaction with nature, an awareness of her controlling influence along with a sensitivity to her vulnerability, holds the key to what this landscape has to offer.

The tantalizing beauty of the place overwhelms people who have spent a lifetime here, as well as first-time visitors. But it is a fragile beauty. It must be protected.

A single lifetime isn't enough to take all the pleasure the mountains have to give. But there is another type of taking. On the one hand there are greedy people who seem determined to undermine every attempt by environmentalists to preserve the wild beauty of the West. On the other there are those who understand that being in the mountains is a privilege.

Fortunately, the majority of the people who live here are in the latter group. It's one of the reasons why they live here. The common thread that binds them together is a good-natured attitude – good-natured in every sense of the word. The understanding that nature is important makes the thread resilient to pressure and opposition and it is an incredibly strong thread. It has made the people capable of fighting for what they believe.

Fortunately, the massive migration to the West in recent years has been joined by people who want to retain the gifts of nature. By and large, the newcomers bring an empathy for the land and all the creatures inhabiting it, and the battle against those who don't have such feelings has become easier. But it's a battle our grandchildren will have to fight as well. Not only are there riches under the ground that will always lure the greedy, but there are insensitive, uncaring people who can damage the landscape simply out of sheer ignorance.

Forest fires are possibly the greatest of all things that menace the environment of the Rockies. Ironically, the factor that raises the danger is the very thing that makes the mountains such a perfect vacationland: Colorado has about three hundred days of golden sunshine a year. The result is that humidity levels are low and the forests are extremely dry for much of the time.

But if the bright sun plays a part in endangering the wilderness, it also adds to the enjoyment for modern man. When the Indians were the only people here, the sun inspired awe and the Utes believed that it could give a man supernatural powers. The Sun Dance, which their descendants still perform for visitors at the only Indian reservation in Colorado, in the southwestern corner of the state, was an annual event for men who wanted to gain some of those powers.

The Sun Dance was a five-day event held in mid-July when the sun was considered to be most powerful. The braves, who were not allowed to eat or drink for the duration of the ceremony, gathered in a circular pen that was made of tree branches. A tall pole topped with a bundle of branches was the focal point of the ceremony and no dancer ever took his eyes off it. Each dancer was given a space along the outer wall with an individual path leading toward the pole in the center and each spent the five days alternately moving backward and forward along his designated path. When they got to the pole, they stayed there for a few minutes gesturing and chanting and communicating with the sun. Usually on the trip back and forth they announced their presence by chanting and blowing whistles made of eagle bones. At some point during the ceremony, whether from hunger, from fatigue or from some sort of self-intoxication, the brave would eventually fall down in a faint. When that happened it was said that they had accumulated all of the sun's power they were capable of absorbing. Naturally the last one to swoon was considered the most powerful.

Modern man draws power from the sun and the Rocky Mountain setting in quite a different way. There is no need to chant, no reason to blow a whistle made of eagle bones. Nothing more is required of you than to stand quietly and look around. What could be more profound than a fresh snowfall, the intricately woven web of a spider, a newborn colt or the natural color of a wildflower? The ambiance of the Rockies is nothing less than exquisite and filled with wonders enough for a lifetime of contemplation.

But there are more people than ever before sharing the experience and the effect of that sometimes upsets the natural balance of the ecosystem and results in an exploitation of the integrity of the land. The mountains that for generations were just a far-off image of splendor for most Americans are now an easy reality for the majority. It is more important than ever to preserve them, before the encroachment of development destroys what nature has given us.

An awareness of the idyllic and untainted beauty of the mountains has become a trademark of a true Westerner. People who live here are as proud of this clean, unexploited environment as were the Indians who worshipped it. Instead of attempting to conquer it, the Indians chose to make friends with it and to become as one with the Almighty God who created it for them. The white man forced the Indians further west beyond the mountains, considering such a wonderful place too good for so-called savages. Now new arrivals are causing alarm about overcrowding.

Expulsion of the Indians from their mountain home was to be incredibly easy. Though they knew very well how to fight, and often did, they were a passive and peaceful people. They lived a life of serenity, in harmony with nature, which the early settlers took advantage of, but which modern Coloradoans are adopting more and more as their own attitude. With a little luck and plenty of care, this time the story will have a different ending.

The mountains rewarded the Indians with rich clay for their pottery, abundant wildlife for their food and that ever-present sun for their inspiration.

The sun shines through five of every six days, splashing the landscape with a brilliant yellow color that rivals anything any artist could paint. It is a net that holds you and keeps you from ever escaping the lure of the Rockies.

In fact, it is only because the mountains are so enticing and the sunshine so inviting that Westerners succumb to the call that holds them here. The majesty of nature makes you aware of the brevity of life; it causes you to reflect on your priorities and to act on immediate impulses. At the core of the Western spirit is a state of mind that allows you to appreciate the moment and the special freedom it grants you. Westerners feel a need to see and do everything quickly and at the same time to absorb the aesthetics that nature has so generously and elaborately bestowed on them. The options are so diverse, so versatile, so numerous, that Coloradoans expend most of their energy outdoors, enjoying the open spaces and the scenic plethora of puzzling delights that give compelling reasons to meditate on the underlying meaning of the universe. It is a normal human undertaking, but in Colorado it is more intense than almost anywhere else. Our minds can wonder, our bodies can rejoice and our senses celebrate. The beauty of the West is that intense.

The Indians often referred to the Rockies as their "Shining Mountains." The Spaniards were impressed by another quality and named the place Colorado, actually because of the Colorado River, whose waters have a red color that makes it memorable. As they explored it, though, they discovered that the countryside itself abounded in other beautiful colors, vibrant and explosive colors that still dazzle the eye.

The color of the land is an exquisite blend of natural tones, ranging from sage green to rust and the deep color of clay. The textures, too, are varied and the variety of geological wonders includes mountains composed entirely of red iron, plateaux thick with clay sediment, deep, dark canyons and majestic rocks that lure climbers of every stripe.

The power that the place held for the early conquistadores still exists as people continue to be mesmerized by the infinite beauty that is unique to this part of the world.

And why not? It is, as they say, "a picture no artist could paint." How could anything be more emphatic, yet more difficult to recreate on canvas, than a full harvest moon rising over a snow-covered field? Only God could produce a more pleasing combination of colors than can be seen in a purple and violet columbine blowing in the warm breeze wafting across an alpine meadow. And what could be more symbolic of the bounty of nature than a fat, orange pumpkin in a windswept wheat field?

The sounds of life are there, too. A blue jay singing on a lofty pine, the distant howl of a coyote reverberating off a canyon wall, the simple sound of the wind blowing through the trees in the high mountains make us all want to silence our own voices and listen to this great force, the secret language of nature whispering delicately at times, roaring fiercely at other times.

It is clearly the place to be for nature lovers and sports enthusiasts alike. The infinitely optimistic soul willing to bare heart and mind to the elements, which often seem hostile, but always compensate for the struggle with lavish rewards, understands very well what winning is all about. There is no place on earth that can boast the combination of the good, soul-satisfying aspects of life in Colorado and the Rockies.

There is urbanity here, too, in great cities like Denver and the other communities that line Colorado's Front Range, but the good, natural life is always at hand. The air is invigorating and gives people a feeling of good health. The mountain slopes that provide the best skiing in the United States in the winter months are transformed in summer into islands of milk and honey as melted snow cascades down the hillsides to the delight of hikers and climbers. Of course, in the high mountain country the snow rarely melts and summer, by the standards of many, never comes.

In the days of the great gold fever in the middle of the last century, a lot of men became the first to explore some of those high places. Those who stayed behind were as curious about the climate as they were about the opportunity to get rich. When an old prospector stumbled into Denver in the fall of 1861, the first question he was asked was about the summer temperatures up there. "I don't know what summer's like in the mountains,' he said, "I wasn't there but eighteen months."

A man could get lost up there, even today, in spite of marked trails, paved roads and helpful neighbors.

Colorado is big. At 104,247 square miles, it is the eighth largest state. Its population of 2,889,735 ranks it twenty-eighth among the fifty United States. Its borders make drawing maps of it child's play. It is a perfect rectangle, with its east-west border extending for four hundred miles, the north-south line for three hundred miles.

And though Colorado is mountainous, a good deal of the state is composed of level plains and valleys that extend some two hundred miles west from the prairies to the foothills of the Rockies where, in a band not more than thirty-five miles wide, about two-thirds of all the people live. Beyond the foothills, fifty-one mountain peaks more than 14,000 feet high are part of the landscape. The most visible from a distance is Pike's Peak, a piker compared to some (it ranks twenty eighth among Colorado's mountains) because it is only 14,110 feet high. It is so dramatic because it rises straight up without any other surrounding high mountains. When Zebulon Pike, the man who is credited with discovering it, first saw it, he wasn't sure it was a mountain at all, but said in his journal that he had seen a mysterious blue cloud on the horizon.

Fifteen hundred of Colorado's mountains are more than 10,000 feet high, which makes it the highest of all states, including Alaska. Its mean altitude is 6,800 feet, over 1,500 feet more than a mile above sea level. The highest point is Mount Elbert, 14,431 feet, which is not far from the lowest point in the state at Holly, near the Kansas border, where the elevation is 3,385 feet. The vertical difference between the two spots is well over two miles.

People are fond of calling Colorado the "Switzerland of America" and, indeed, there are colonies of Swiss-Americans who have come here because of the comfort of familiarity. But the name was probably dreamed up by the Swiss Tourist Office. The fact is, Colorado has six times the mountain area of Switzerland and the fabled Matterhorn is only 250 feet higher than Mount Elbert.

Just as Colorado is more than the Rockies, the Rocky Mountains cover a good deal more territory than Colorado. In the United States, the mountains stretch over ten states; from Idaho and Montana in the north to the southern reaches of New Mexico and Arizona. The extreme distances that separate those states have had a distinctive effect on social, economic and cultural development. A Coloradoan is as different from someone who has grown up in northern Wyoming as they both are from a native of southern Utah. But the Westerners have a lot of things in common, perhaps the most important of which is that they aren't at all like the natives of the East Coast.

To compare East and West in the United States is like trying to mix oil and water. And the more you try, the more you emphasize the differences. The main emphasis in the West is placed on youth and the freedom it lives for. James A. Michener described it as: "its wild joy in living, its vital experimentalism in the arts and its willingness to cultivate new industries and new ways of doing old jobs." The Eastern view of it all, fortunately, has changed somewhat since Daniel Webster's day when he described the West as "a worthless area." There is a good reason for that. If Webster could see what has become of the West, he would collapse in surprise. It was a region of incomparable beauty then, but the beauty is only part of the story these days. If he considered "worth" to be related to natural resources, he'd surely retract the question posed in 1852: "What use could we ever hope to put these great deserts and these endless mountain ranges?"

Consider this, Daniel Webster:

A metal called molybdenum, which is used to harden steel, and is the very best metal for making rockets, is found in abundance in the Colorado Rockies – half the world's supply, in fact. Some forty per cent of the coal deposits in the entire United States are under "these endless mountain ranges." Oil is down there, too, in the hardened clay they call shale. In terms of personal income, Mr. Webster, people who live in your native New Hampshire today earn an average of $10,073 per year. In Colorado, the average is $11,142.

But Daniel Webster could have been forgiven for all of that. What did he know about molybdenum or shale oil? How could he have known that Colorado would some day become a center for publishing and printing and the manufacture of electrical equipment? But if he had only lived six more years, he might have bought a wagon and headed west.

In the winter of 1858, word began to spread that the Russell brothers, a family of gold miners from Georgia, had struck it rich along Cherry Creek. By the following March, the parade had begun. The area was vaguely known in those days as "Pike's Peak Country" and the wagons following the Platte River across the plains carried huge signs that shouted, "Pike's Peak or Bust." Not one of them intended to "bust" of course. There was gold in "them thar hills." One of the people who told them so was no less a person than Horace Greeley, editor of *The New York Tribune*, who made an inspection trip of what he called "the Kansas gold fields" in the spring of 1859. He went to a camp named Central City, not far west of Denver, and was astounded to report, in the first "entry" of *The Rocky Mountain News*, that the population of 4,000 (including five white women and seven Indian squaws) was composed of people who had been there less than a month and that at least five hundred more were arriving every day. The newcomers, he said, were "… sleeping in tents or under pine boughs, cooking and eating in the open (on a diet of) pork, hot bread, beans and coffee." But he noted that "a meat shop has just been established, on whose altar are offered up the ill-fed and well-whipped oxen who are just in from a fifty-day journey across the plains." In spite of all that, the best advice he could offer his readers back in New York was to "go West, young man!"

Greeley gave an honest report of what he saw in the Colorado mountains and he did see a lot of gold. But he tempered his report with warnings that the hard winters could make the mining season short and that the rugged countryside would make getting at the gold a tough proposition. He was also careful to point out that gold mining was no game for amateurs. But that didn't stop the hordes of young men from heading west, a fact that made *The New York Times*, Greeley's arch rival, wring its hands and point out that the power of the *Tribune's* printed words would surely cause nothing but suffering and break up happy homes, not to mention filling New York's poorhouses to the rafters.

There was no need for a poorhouse in Denver City in 1859. It had a hotel, though. It was a log cabin. It didn't have any beds, but if you had a blanket you could sleep on the floor. Horace Greeley called it "The Astor House," because its rates were the same as the hotel he knew so well on Fifth Avenue back in New York. It cost more to have a drink out here (twenty-five cents a shot for pure alcohol with flavoring added), but Greeley didn't indulge. In fact, the original intention of his western junket was to deliver temperance lectures.

Actually, in those days there were two cities on the banks of

Cherry Creek and rivalry between them was so strong that when *The Rocky Mountain News* began publication in 1859, it had its office built on pilings in the middle of the creek in an effort not to take sides or to lose valuable circulation. The city on the western bank was called Auraria and if Denver City had a hotel, it boasted a school; the first "on the frontier of civilization." It was started by a man named O.J. Goldrick, who startled the prospectors in 1859 when he arrived in town wearing a silk hat, a frock coat and yellow kid gloves. He had two college degrees and papers to prove it. But he had no paper money. His net worth after the trip across the plains was just fifty cents. That's where the silk hat comes in. He passed it among the miners, asking for donations for education, and in a matter of minutes collected $250. A few weeks later he opened the doors of the Union School, which on that first day had an enrollment of thirteen. His neighbors considered it a lucky day anyway, and used his enterprise as a means of luring new settlers to their town. They met every wagon train and proudly announced: "We have a school!"

It was indeed something to be proud of, but the city across the creek was growing faster. By 1860, Denver had its first skyscraper, a commercial building three stories high. Between them, Auraria and Denver had eight hotels, but the best were conceded to be on the Denver side. The Aurarians tried hard to compete with their sister city across the creek, but it was a losing battle. Things came to a head when entrepreneurs slightly to the west began tub-thumping for a new city of the future – the little town of Golden, whose very name was a promoter's dream. Seeing the writing on the wall, the city fathers of Auraria agreed to a merger with Denver. The marriage was consummated on April 5th, 1860, in an after-dark ceremony in the middle of the bridge between the two towns. The name they kept, of course, was Denver, but the Aurarians were allowed to keep a semblance of a separate identity by being called "Denver, West Division."

The name Auraria was removed forever from the map of Colorado that day, but its namesake is still home to some three hundred souls in the Blue Ridge Mountains of northern Georgia. The name Denver was given to the mining camp on the banks of Cherry Creek by a delegation of settlers from Kansas who agreed it would be a politically wise gesture to honor the Governor of the Kansas Territory, of which this was a part in those days. What they didn't know was that between the time they left Kansas and came up with a name for their settlement, James W. Denver had been replaced as governor of the Territory.

There is still gold in those hills, but it isn't a major industry or even a growth factor in Colorado anymore. Yet every once in a while an adventurer shows up looking for lost caches of gold. There are legends all over the place and enough old-timers to keep them alive. Two of them are similar enough to make you wonder about all the rest. The first involves a group of Spanish prospectors who showed up after the turn of the nineteenth century and struck it very rich in the southeastern part of the state. One of them got even luckier. He married the daughter of an Araphaho chief. He had no sooner settled down to enjoy life with his princess, however, than the Utes and the Araphahoes went to war. The chief recommended that his son-in-law and his friends leave for the duration of the conflict, so they packed their gold onto the backs of burros and headed for the southwest. They hadn't gone far when they spotted a Ute war party. It was obvious they'd be dead if they didn't get rid of the gold they were carrying, so they buried the treasure – several dozen fifty-pound gold bars – under a rock. Then, after marking the spot with an old shovel, they raced off as fast as their horses could carry them for the safety of New Spain.

Rather than go back to Colorado, they eventually sailed back to the Old Country and their gold stayed buried behind them. A dozen years later, the Spaniard, having a wife in Colorado, went back, but discovered his bride was dead. She had left him a beautiful young daughter, though, and he dedicated the rest of his life to making her happy, never once mentioning his buried treasure until the day he died. The daughter didn't care much for gold and promptly forgot about it. Years later she casually mentioned it to her son, who wasn't nearly as casual about the prospect of being a millionaire. The only problem was that by the time he found the right field full of boulders, he couldn't find the right rock because the shovel was long gone. He never did find it. Nor has anyone else.

Another story revolves around an 1880s prospector who wandered into Denver with a report of a hidden mine not far from Sangre de Cristo Pass. He said it was so carefully hidden that nobody would ever find it without following the instructions he had written in his will, which left the mine and its treasure to his sister. The key to the instructions was a pick he said he had embedded into a tree root with its handle pointing to the mine's secret entrance. His sister couldn't find it. Nor could any of a dozen searching parties spurred on by the publicity her plight had generated. Someone had taken the pick. That was in 1884. The mine, with piles of gold dust just inside the entrance, hasn't been found since.

True stories? Who knows? And there are others. Some say there are a dozen chests of Spanish gold at the bottom of the Purgatory River and an Aztec treasure at the bottom of "Bottomless Lake" in Mustang Canyon. There's a cave, they say, somewhere in Colorado, that is filled with Spanish treasure. Explorers thought they had found that one back in the 1930s because someone spotted a cross carved in a rock that might point them in the right direction. But when they went back for more careful exploration, people with guns who used the rocks for target practice had blasted the cross away and had pitted enough other rocks to make identification impossible.

With or without the help of vandals, the mountains hold many secrets. Hundreds of millions of years ago the entire area was covered by enormous seas, which is the reason why parts of Colorado look very much like tidal flats to people who come from coastal regions. They once were. As the seas receded, they were replaced alternately by subtropical forests and deserts. At various times, the seas came back, each time leaving a different legacy. Some five hundred million years ago, for instance, the ocean left behind a wasteland, and underground forces pushing rocks to the surface gave us the beautiful, multicolored rocks that make a trip to the Garden of the Gods in Colorado Springs so memorable. Constantly changing levels of the water stratified them with a wonderful shade of red, accented by greens, grays and whites.

It all took so long that our understanding of time in terms of eons isn't adequate. At various times it was an area of lush, dinosaur-infested forests and a harsh land that supported no life at all. But it is generally agreed that the mountains as we know them today were formed at the end of what geologists call the Mesozoic Era, which occured, give or take a few thousand years, about eighty million years ago. At that time a combination of earthquakes and volcanic activity gradually pushed the mountains up from the plain. Underground rocks were hurled to the surface and granite was tilted upward to form awesome crags and peaks. Meanwhile, lava poured from every convenient opening and then cooled to form solid rock.

Once that excitement was over, nature began a refining process. Wind and water conspired to wear down the rough edges, to fill in gaps with left-over volcanic ash that covered the nearby prairie, and to carve out canyons and gorges. Glaciers came and went and contributed to the process, leaving behind moraines and deposits of loose rock.

The Rocky Mountain system is subdivided into a northern and a southern range, and is again divided by broken plateaux extending from the Wyoming basin to the Snake River Plain. North and west of Yellowstone National Park in Wyoming and Montana, the Northern Rockies extend all the way north to Alaska. The Southern Rockies are considered by many to be less spectacular because they don't have the same concentration of massive spires and there are no ridges on the upturned foothills. The Southern Rockies are mainly a series of long ridges with upturned sediment layers on each side.

There is a north-south division to the Rockies, too. It is called the Continental Divide. Technically, the Divide marks the middle of the mountains, and rivers and streams flowing down the western slope eventually find their way to the Pacific Ocean, while water on the other side flows east to eventually empty into the Atlantic. The Divide isn't a straight line, by any means. In Colorado, it crosses the Wyoming border at the top of the Park Range, but then soon cuts to the east along the Rabbit Ears Range. After running east for about fifty miles, it turns south again and cuts through Rocky Mountain National Park. Then it heads southwest, where it passes the headwaters of the eastbound Arkansas River, the westbound Colorado River and the southbound Rio Grande. It finally crosses the San Juan Mountains on its way to New Mexico.

Although the Continental Divide runs along the most spectacular of mountains, some of Colorado's more dramatic summits, like Pikes Peak and Longs Peak, are not part of it.

But the Rockies are not all towering peaks and bottomless canyons. Everywhere, especially directly under the tallest of the mountains, there are natural parklands, farms and ranches nestled on plateaux and in deep valleys. While the mountains may have seemed like an unconquerable barrier to early settlers, they gradually planted themselves here anyway. The soil is rich in many places. The forests are abundant with fur-bearing animals. There is a wealth of minerals underground. For all those reasons, it was worthwhile the settlers making their peace with nature.

Gradually they found ways around the high mountains, and where there was no way, they either enlarged existing passes or constructed new ones in the high mountains. In later years, they even dared to build railroads through them on passes at elevations ranging from 7,500 to 12,000 feet. Explorers and builders have found five hundred passes to help avoid climbing up and over the Rockies. There are 136 of them in Colorado.

Though the majority of the first settlers came to get rich, even those who never came close to realizing their dreams never went home again. The climate was better here.

Back in the days when the Pilgrims were grumbling about the weather in Massachusetts, the Spaniards were at work with their unique ways of bringing civilization to the Indians in Colorado. The Indians had never seen anything like the conquistadores, but then, the Spaniards had never seen anything like the Rockies, where Indians had been living for 20,000 years. The Smithsonian Institution has uncovered arrowheads north of Denver that are at least that old, and spearheads have been found among the bones of a type of bison that became extinct more than 10,000 years ago.

But the modern Indians that the Spaniards found lived their lives in a way much different from their prehistoric ancestors. The modern era in the Red Man's terms began in about 800 AD, when a race of farmers appeared in southwestern Colorado. They weren't warlike, but their neighbors were, so to defend themselves they built their homes in the walls of canyons. These early apartment houses were high up out of harm's way and featured large rooms capable of holding enough food and water to withstand long sieges. Some of the best-preserved remains of these pueblos are in Mesa Verde National Park, where scientists estimate the culture flourished until the end of the thirteenth century, when they were possibly starved out in a great drought that lasted twenty years. They left behind so many clues about themselves that anthropologists can say with certainty that they suffered from bad teeth, often had stomach troubles and that rheumatism was a constant complaint.

By the time the white man began making his presence known, Colorado was populated by seven different tribes of Utes, part of the Shoshone Nation, and in the plains by the Kiowa, Comanche, Araphaho and Cheyenne. Though the plains Indians were cousins in the Algonquin family, they didn't get along too well with each other and were constantly at war. Occasionally they dragged the Ute into their disputes, but with the mountains for an ally, the latter were virtually invincible.

The wars between the tribes were fairly constant anyway. The plains Indians were not the sort to give up. The result was that, although they were not warlike, the Ute were good fighters and that, they thought, was an asset when the white man came.

In the years when Philadelphia was still a small town, the Colorado Utes and their Navajo neighbors in the southwest joined in a conspiracy to harass the Spanish and kept at it for 150 years. They settled their dispute with New Spain in 1858 and for the next ten years contented themselves with an occasional raid on ranchers and prospectors who were moving in on them.

The government in Washington solved this particular "Indian problem" with one of its famous treaties in 1868. Under its terms, the Ute were moved into the southwestern part of the Territory. But five years later it was discovered that there were minerals under the Indian territory and the Government moved them again. Those considered hostile were transferred to a reservation in Utah, the meeker ones were given a reservation in the southwestern corner in an area that nobody else wanted. Their descendants are still there.

In the meantime, the Comanche, who like the Utes were a Shoshone tribe, were forced out of their home in the Black Hills of South Dakota after a war with the Sioux. They moved into southern Colorado, which they used as a base for raiding parties into New Mexico and Texas, where they enjoyed the enviable reputation of being the fiercest of all Indians. Other tribes steered a wide berth around them – even their cousins, the Utes.

Then a tribe even more bloodthirsty appeared on the scene, the Kiowa. After battling with each other for several years, the Kiowa and Comanche finally forged an alliance and then extended the hand of friendship to the Cheyenne and Araphaho. All four Indian nations bonded themselves together in 1840 and for nearly thirty years defended their hunting grounds against the white man's "Manifest Destiny."

"Manifest Destiny" was the white man's way of justifying the great move to the West in spite of the fact there were people there already. It was the will of God, they said, and heaven protect anyone who got in the way.

In Washington there was another justification. President Thomas Jefferson had purchased the area in 1803 for four cents an acre. He bought it from Napoleon who claimed he owned it because French explorers had discovered it first.

Even Napoleon didn't know what was out there. He had once planned to attack the British in Canada from the Pacific Northwest, but then decided to sell the land instead. Jefferson knew he had made a good bargain, but he wasn't sure how vast this new territory was and so, in his role as Commander-in-Chief, he ordered a troop of sixteen soldiers to march out from St. Louis to find the source of both the Arkansas and Red rivers. It was vital information to him because Napoleon had sold him all the territory west of the Mississippi River, but the territory in the southwest hadn't been his to sell. It was "owned" by Spain. Jefferson needed to fix the southern boundary of the area the French called "Louisiana."

The little band of soldiers was led by Captain Zebulon Montgomery Pike, who had been born and raised in New Jersey, but had earned a reputation on the plains as a tough Indian fighter. He had a good reputation as an explorer, too, having spent ten years exploring the Mississippi. His party arrived in Colorado in the winter of 1806, lured by a mysterious blue cloud that turned out to be Pike's Peak. True to his instincts as an explorer, Captain Pike set out to climb the mountain, but he hadn't gotten far when a blizzard struck and he was forced back. Claiming that no man would ever be able to climb that mountain, he moved on to the south, looking for the Red River, which the Louisiana Purchase stipulated as the southern boundary of French territory. What he found instead was the Rio Grande, a mistake that was driven home when he found himself surrounded by Spanish soldiers who hustled him off to Santa Fe. He never did find the Red River and the boundary wasn't established until 1861, when a treaty agreed it would be the Arkansas River on the south and the Continental Divide on the west.

Washington still wasn't sure what it had gotten for its money and in 1820, President James Monroe dispatched another group of soldiers to have a look around. This one was commanded by Major Stephen H. Long, who didn't think anything good would ever come of the flat country at the edge of the mountains. The historian attached to the party, Dr. Edwin James, put another myth to rest by climbing to the top of Pike's Peak, even though Pike had said no one ever would.

Both Pike and Long confirmed what the Spanish and the Indians had been saying all along: that the Sangre de Cristo range is among the most beautiful of all the Rocky Mountains. The difference was that these people kept journals which became the basis for newspaper articles and books calculated to fire the imaginations of the folks back East.

It was part of the game. The territory wasn't even worth four cents an acre unless people could be encouraged to settle there. Governments don't control territory, they control people.

Knowledge of the high mountains had already been recorded and expanded by the Lewis and Clark expedition of 1804. Jefferson had sent Meriwether Lewis and William Clark to figure out if there was a convenient way to get to Oregon across those mountains. They went out by way of Montana, but came back through Wyoming because they found the Indians in the north a bit too hostile for comfort. Their southern return route eventually became the Oregon Trail, which made it convenient, in a manner of speaking, for settlers to go west. Their journals, too, provided a public relations tool to make the move seem attractive.

Word that civilized life was possible in the high mountains was heard in the south, too, in the territory known as New Spain. After the boundaries of the Louisiana Purchase were settled, about two-thirds of present-day Colorado had become officially Spanish. The rest was called Louisiana. When Texas won its independence from Mexico in 1863, western Colorado became part of the Lone Star State. But Mexico disagreed. After Texas was admitted to the Union, the United States and Mexico decided that war was the only way to settle the dispute. When the smoke cleared, the U.S. had clear title to all of Colorado, but agreed to respect the rights of all Mexicans living there. Following the rule that the only valid territory is a colonized territory, the Mexican Government had anticipated the war by granting huge tracts of Colorado land to its citizens. In this way, the million-acre Sangre de Cristo grant became home to six families who, in 1851, founded the town of San Luis, the first permanent settlement in Colorado. Three years later another group founded Conejos on the Continental Divide side of the San Luis Valley. They were the ancestors of the largest ethnic minority in Colorado today – the Chicanos. There are about 200,000 of them in the state now, adding a very special touch to the human landscape. The Chicanos are actually a blend of two distinct groups – Indian and Spanish – and they cling to the traditions of both. They represent one of the reasons why Colorado's heritage is as colorful as it is.

As colorful as Colorado and her people are today, nothing anywhere quite compares to the people who once roamed the area in search of beaver skins. They called them "mountain men."

From the beginning of the seventeenth century until near the end of the nineteenth, no self-respecting gentleman in either

Europe or the United States was considered worthy of the name if he didn't possess a beaver hat. Every lady had a fur shawl and both sexes favored fur trim on their coats. It was big business.

In the early days of American settlement, trappers cut corners by hiring Indians to bring back skins for them. But by the time the frontier moved to the Rockies, the big fur buyers had established a preference for white trappers. Indians were too unreliable, they said.

At first glance you might mistake one of these mountain men for an Indian. Long months in the sun turned their skin the color of leather and what the sun didn't accomplish, a combination of soot and bear grease did.

To say they never washed wouldn't be quite true. Beaver traps had to be set under water, after all. But scraggly hair was almost as much a mountain man's trademark as the fringed buckskin clothes he wore. His shoes were moccasins made of deer skin or buffalo hide and often, when times got tough, they doubled as a meal.

Every mountain man carried a long butcher's knife in his belt, along with a pair of pistols. He carried his ammunition, about a pound of lead balls, in a pouch around his neck and the powder to fire it in a horn over his shoulder. Other tools of his trade were in a pouch draped over the other shoulder and he carried a heavy rifle, usually about .60-caliber, in his hands. The guns were of a special type made in St. Louis and were capable of dropping a moving buffalo from as far away as two hundred yards.

In addition to his tools, he carried extra powder and lead, adding over a hundred pounds of extra weight. He packed a pipe and tobacco, a bit of flour, some coffee and some salt. The rest of his food he picked up along the way in the form of nuts and berries and any sort of animal or bird that might cross his path. He also had a half dozen or so traps, but once they were in place he didn't have to carry them around with him.

Trapping was a seasonal business. The first run of the year began in the fall when the animals were beginning to get their winter coats, and continued into winter until the ice got too thick to get at the traps. The second season started when the ice began to break up and continued until summer weather made the quality of the fur less valuable.

In the winter months between the two seasons, a mountain man wouldn't come down from the hills, but would make camp in a sunny spot protected from the wind and out of sight of wandering Indians. He spent the time preparing his skins and possibly reading. Many carried Bibles, some even carried books of poetry. For many of them it wasn't a completely lonely life. Some bought Indian girls to spend the year with them, for companionship of course, and also to keep the camp ship-shape. After the spring season was over and the skins were ready, trappers from all parts of the mountains came together at a pre-arranged spot for what was known as the annual rendezvous. They stayed there for a month before going back for more skins.

A trapper could easily collect $1,500 for the skins he brought down from the mountains. The companies that bought them from him would generally collect twice that much back in St. Louis. But the companies had other ways of making money. It's one of the reasons why the rendezvous lasted a month.

The wagons that were sent out to collect the pelts weren't sent out empty. They were loaded with trade goods that trappers used to keep the Indians friendly, with whisky that the trappers used to help them forget their troubles and with all the other gear, from tobacco to gunpowder, that every mountain man considered necessities. The merchandise was sold to them at prices hundreds of times over cost.

During the month of the rendezvous even the most frugal trapper would be parted with much of his newly found wealth. But the rendezvous was worth it. After eleven months alone in the wilderness, it was a great adventure just to have someone to talk to. And to drink with. There was gambling to be done, fights to be fought, women to be chased after. The lucky ones who had anything left over at the end of the month usually used what they had to negotiate with the Indians for a girl to take back into the mountains. The price could be as low as a quart of whiskey, which went for about four dollars at a rendezvous, or as high as a dozen beaver pelts, which could bring as much as fifty dollars from a fur trader. It all depended on how young or how pretty the girl might have been. When a man rode off from a rendezvous he was probably already thinking about next year's event. But out there in the mountains there were rattlesnakes and bears, high cliffs and deep ponds, angry snowclouds and hostile men with guns. There were Indians, too, all conspiring against the trapper's chances of remaining alive for the next year's rendezvous.

But if the mortality rate was high, there were always other men anxious to take their place – no matter what else could be said about the life of a mountain man, not one of them ever died of boredom.

Somehow you're never quite alone in the Rocky Mountains. You're in the company of an eagle soaring overhead, a chipmunk scampering out of your path. You're in the company of your own soul, which can communicate with you here as almost nowhere else in the world. Off in the distance, the roar of a waterfall lures you toward it. The sight of it stops your heart. Above you, snowcapped peaks take your breath away. Below you, a cultivated valley satisfies your sense of order. In between a field of wildflowers invites you to run through them, to absorb their scent and revel in their colors. Off in the distance a silvery lake reflects it all in water so clean and clear you could spot a trout twenty feet down. A magnificent elk crosses up ahead, stops for a moment to give you a disdainful look and then moves on as if to say he doesn't care if you exist.

But you care. You're in Colorado, where existence is something special. It's a place where you wish you could stay forever, living a life that would never end.

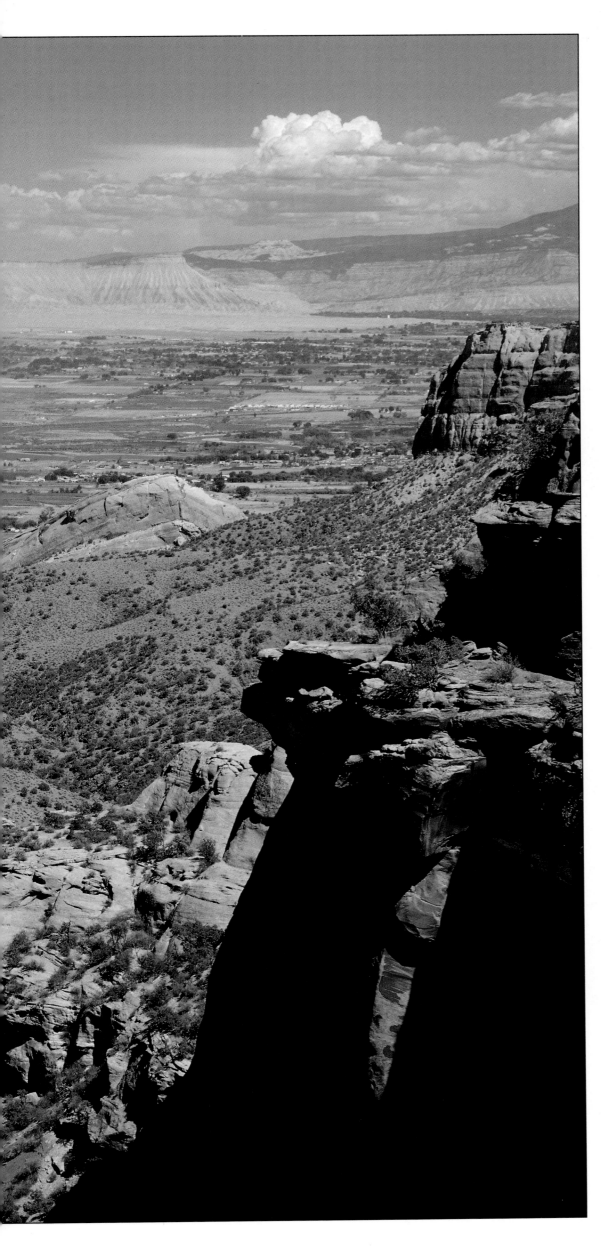

Previous pages: a silver-blue ribbon in the sunlight, the Green River wends its narrow course through Lodore Canyon in Dinosaur National Monument, an area in the extreme northwest of Colorado set aside to preserve the world's largest concentration of fossils, including an impressive number of dinosaur bones. Left: Monument Canyon in Colorado National Monument, south of the town of Grand Junction. The wind-sculpted rocks of this protected area display a bizarre beauty, as well as providing shelter for bobcats and bighorn sheep.

Steamboat Springs (these pages and overleaf) is a north Colorado ski town. Not for nothing is the Centennial State nicknamed "Ski Country" – Steamboat Springs is just one of thirty-five resorts around Colorado dedicated to the sport. The atmosphere in Steamboat is, however, different from that in many other resorts – as a commercial ranching center, it retains a lingering sense of the Wild West. Above: Lincoln Avenue, the town's main street and (above right) Thunderhead Restaurant on the summit of Mount Thunderhead – a welcome sight for skiers (overleaf). Right: a ski-joring contest in downtown Steamboat Springs – Switzerland meets the Wild West!

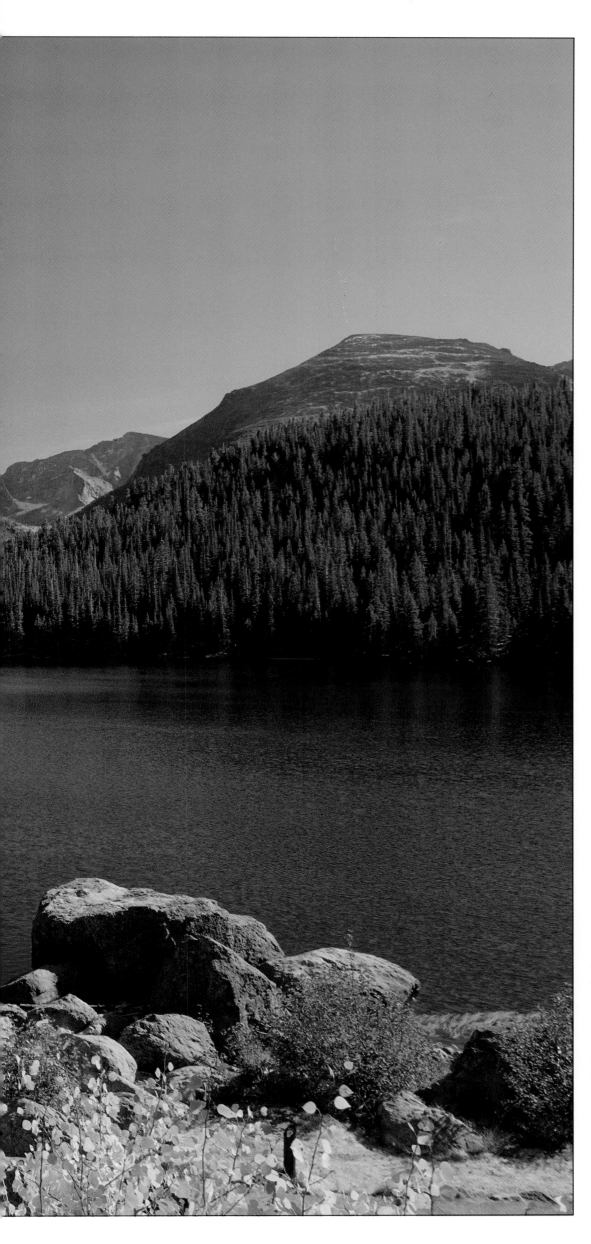

Their color reminiscent of beaten gold, the slightest breath of air shivers slim-stalked aspen leaves ready to fall beside Bear Lake. This lake is one of the most beautifully situated in Rocky Mountain National Park, an extremely popular reserve in northern Colorado that is still lovely in the autumn, when the majority of its annual three million visitors have come and gone. Even in high summer, though, it is possible to get away from the crowds, as the park contains over 300 miles of trails, many of which provide access to the reserve's more remote sections. On these, one is more likely to meet an elk or a black bear than another human being.

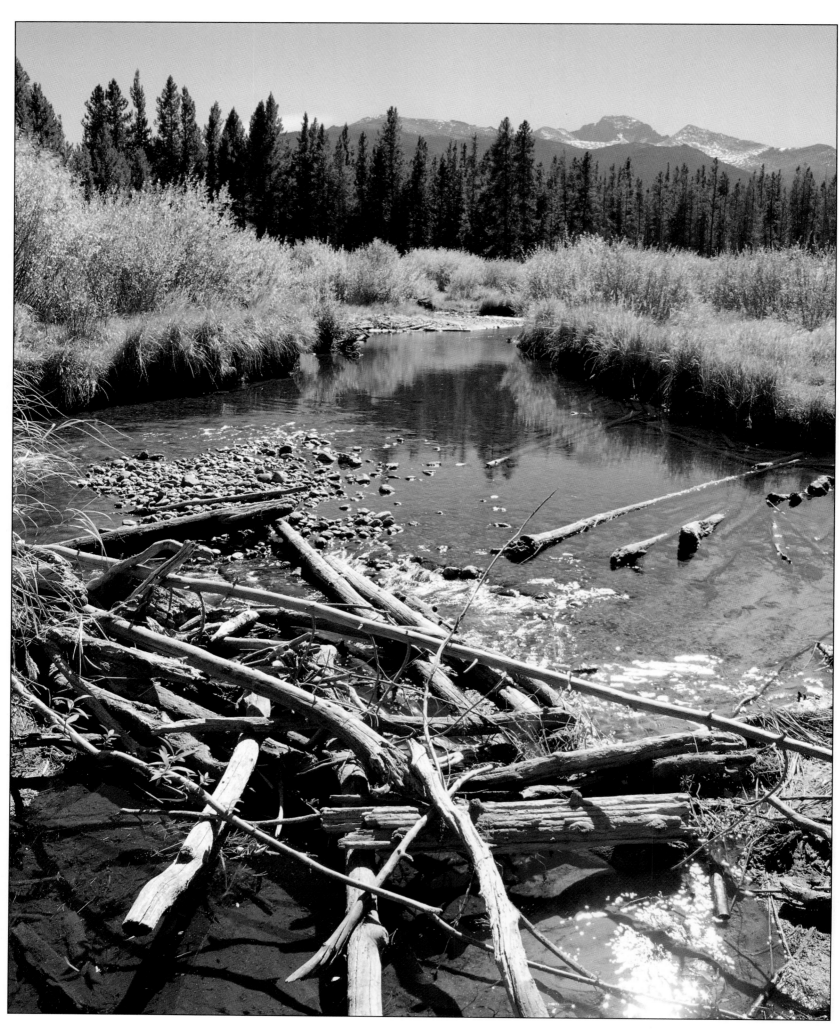

Above: a tangle of branches left high and dry by spring meltwater is bleached white by the sun in Bear Creek, a stream that has its source in Bear Lake in Rocky Mountain National Park. Possibly the fairest tree of this national park's forests, in the fall the sunshine-yellow aspen (facing page) finds the perfect foil in legions of sober-colored conifers. Overleaf: sculptured wood and splintered rock create a primeval atmosphere over Dream Lake, Rocky Mountain National Park.

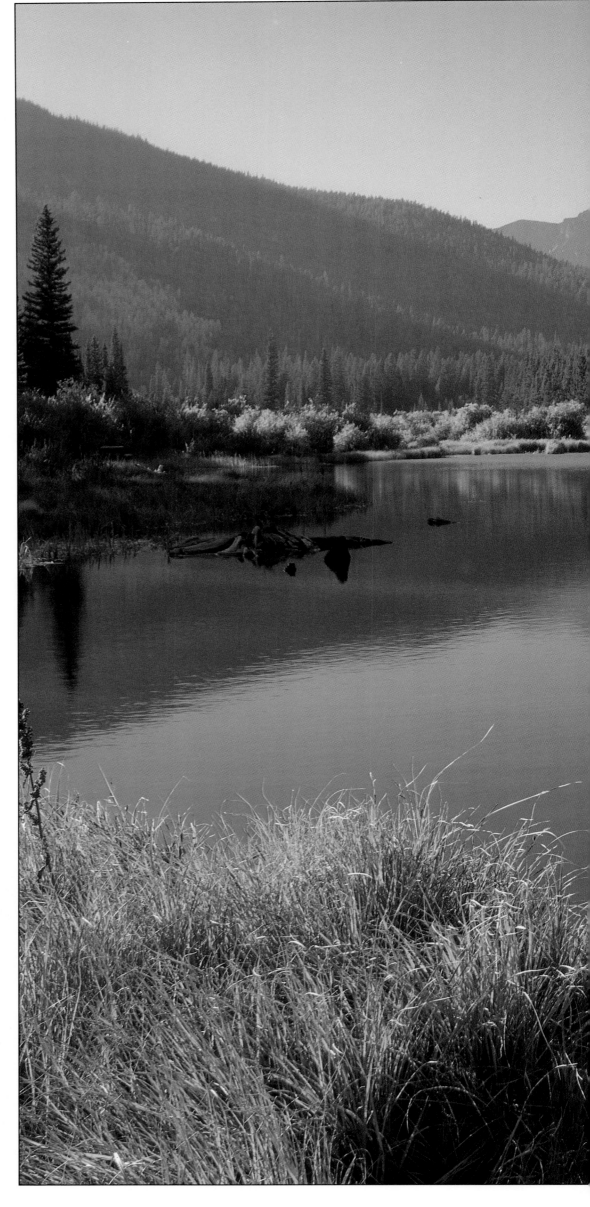

Two hikers pause beside Beaver Ponds, whose intense blues reflect a perfect summer afternoon sky, as, for a moment, the wind holds its breath. The beauty of this lake in Hidden Valley, Rocky Mountains National Park, often goes unnoticed by the majority of the valley's visitors, who arrive in winter when this stretch of water is frozen under deep snow. Hidden Valley Ski Area is the park's center for downhill skiing, cross-country skiing being available in the lower valleys and winter mountaineering in the high country. Overleaf: to the south of Hidden Valley, thick fingers of fir fringe the park's Bear Lake, beyond which the square-jawed bulk of Hallett Peak rises 12,713 feet.

Above left and above: first snow brings the winter colors of ice blue and cool gray to Denver, the state capital and the largest city of Colorado. Left: the metallic glint of Denver's downtown district, the financial center of the state. This district, though it may look forbidding, is designed to be "user friendly" – pedestrian skywalks and bridges make it possible to get around this area without fighting the traffic or adverse weather conditions. It comes as no surprise to discover that it was in this people-orientated city that the shopping mall originated – Denver's version of this convenience is a mile long.

Old Glory flies in front of the Civic Center in Denver (overleaf), a beautifully situated city built a mile above sea level on the banks of the South Platte River and Cherry Creek. Contrary to popular belief, Denver is not actually in the mountains, it is simply near them. The Front Range of the Rocky Mountains rises some thirty miles to the west – Denver itself lies on the Great Plain and is flatter than Manhattan. This situation also benefits the city's climate as bad weather from the west often spends its force in the mountains before reaching Denver. Snow does not stay long here and, in fact, the capital receives about the same amount of rain as Los Angeles and even more hours of sunshine than Miami Beach.

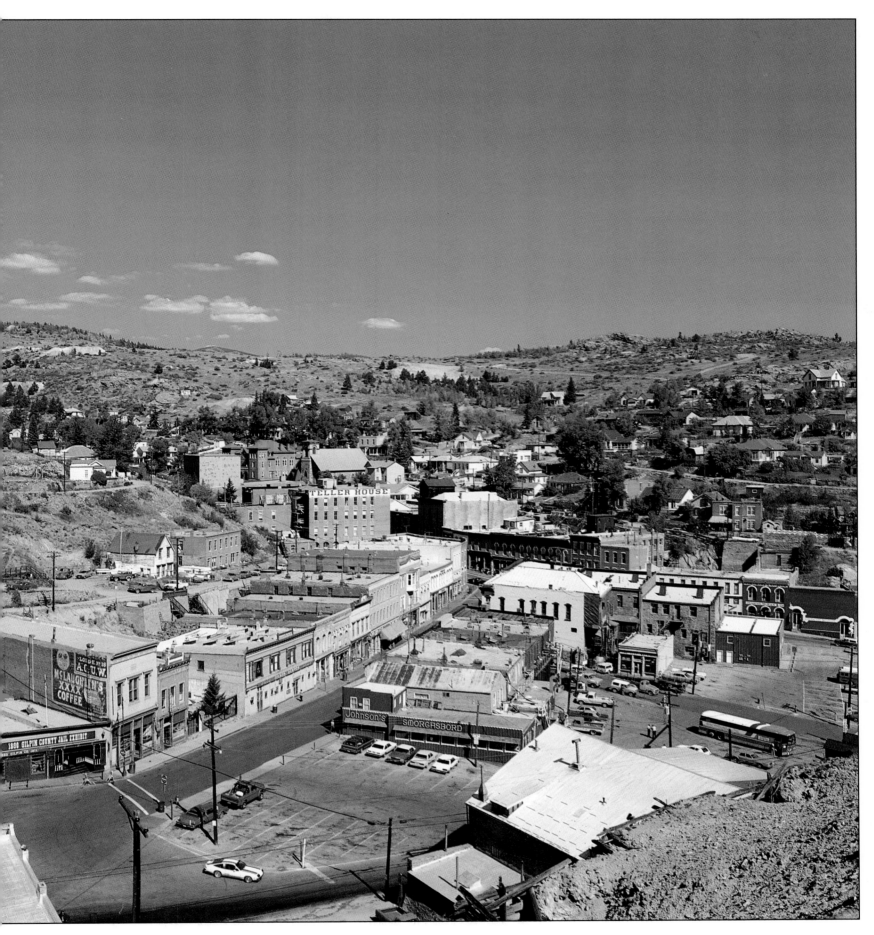

Above: Central City, where a huge gold strike in 1859 was nearly Denver's undoing – upon receipt of news of the strike virtually all the population of the latter downed tools and went west to this town in search of instant wealth. Central City was known for a time as the "richest square mile on earth," with some justification. Since the strike, more than $75 million worth of metal and minerals have been mined in the area. Above left: the Lace House, distinctive for its gingerbread style, in Black Hawk, and (left) Buffalo Bill Cody's grave on Lookout Mountain above the town of Golden, both west of Denver.

Facing page top: the utilitarian kitchen and (bottom) the comparatively rococo dining room of Georgetown's Hotel de Paris, today a museum, but once one of the most elegant hostelries west of the Mississippi. Originally a silver-mining boom town, Georgetown was one of very few such communities not ravaged by fire during the last century. Consequently, much Victorian architecture (above) remains, and the town retains a strong sense of its history.

Deciduous trees, vibrant in their summer livery, zig-zag down a mountain clothed in conifers to cluster beside the Georgetown Loop Railroad. This railway, once a main supply route, is an integral part of the Georgetown-Silver Plume National Historic Landmark, which encompasses and preserves this mining region in the Rockies west of Denver. Both Georgetown and Silver Plume were fabulously wealthy silver-mining towns in their day. A splendid steam locomotive tours the four-mile-long Loop, so called because the track covers the mountainous terrain between Georgetown and Silver Plume by running over and under itself repeatedly on bridges rising six hundred feet above the valley floor.

Above: the prestigious winter resort of Vail awaits the first snows. Vail was created some thirty years ago purely as a ski resort, its back ski bowls being considered the finest on the continent. Today there is much more than skiing to be enjoyed here – golf, scenic gondola rides, river rafting and lawn parties are offered throughout the year to tempt some of the world's wealthiest clientele. Shopping in Vail is definitely a recreational activity, its varied selection of stores being both beautiful and expensive, while for those interested in history the Colorado Ski Museum offers a fascinating exhibition of artifacts that pay tribute to the state's ski industry. Above left: Leadville, a former mining town surrounded by national forest, and (left) a simple dirt track near Dillon, a town centered around Dillon Lake.

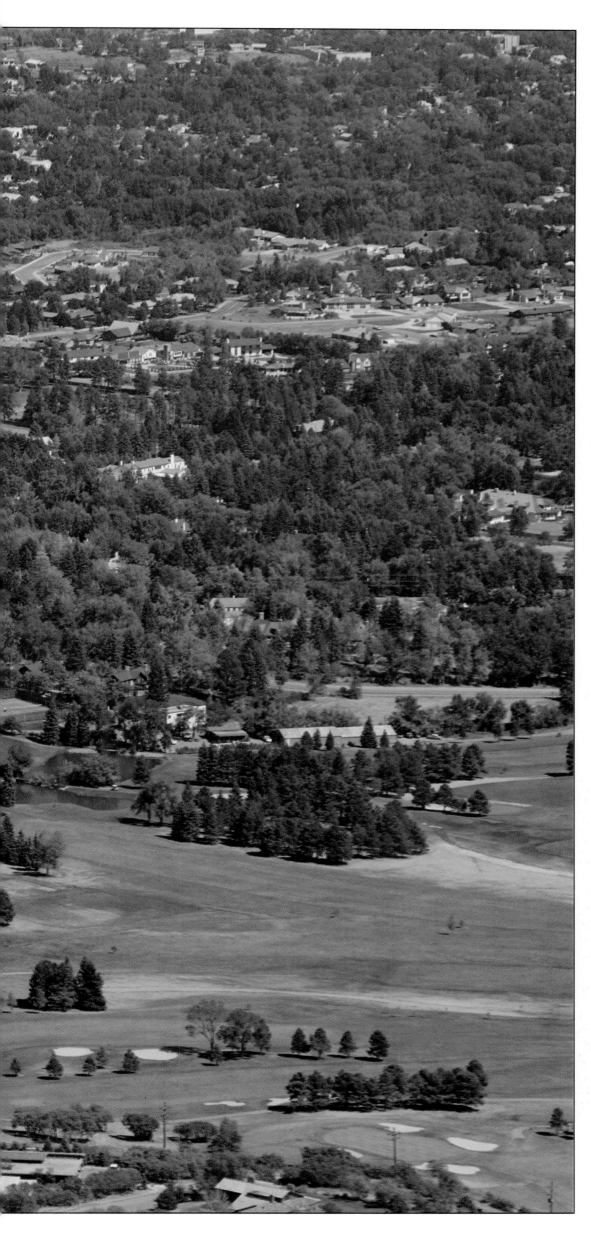

An aerial view of the red roofs and tennis courts of the five-star Broadmoor Hotel complex in Colorado Springs. At the turn of the century this hotel and its casino were bought and renovated by one Spencer Penrose, a wealthy property developer. With an eye to expanding Colorado Springs as a resort – and thereby attracting clients for his hotel – Spencer gave the town a zoo, a polo field, an indoor arena and a library, as well as initiating the construction of the Cheyenne Mountain Highway and the Pike's Peak cog railway. His success in attracting custom was marked – today both the hotel and the resort are world famous.

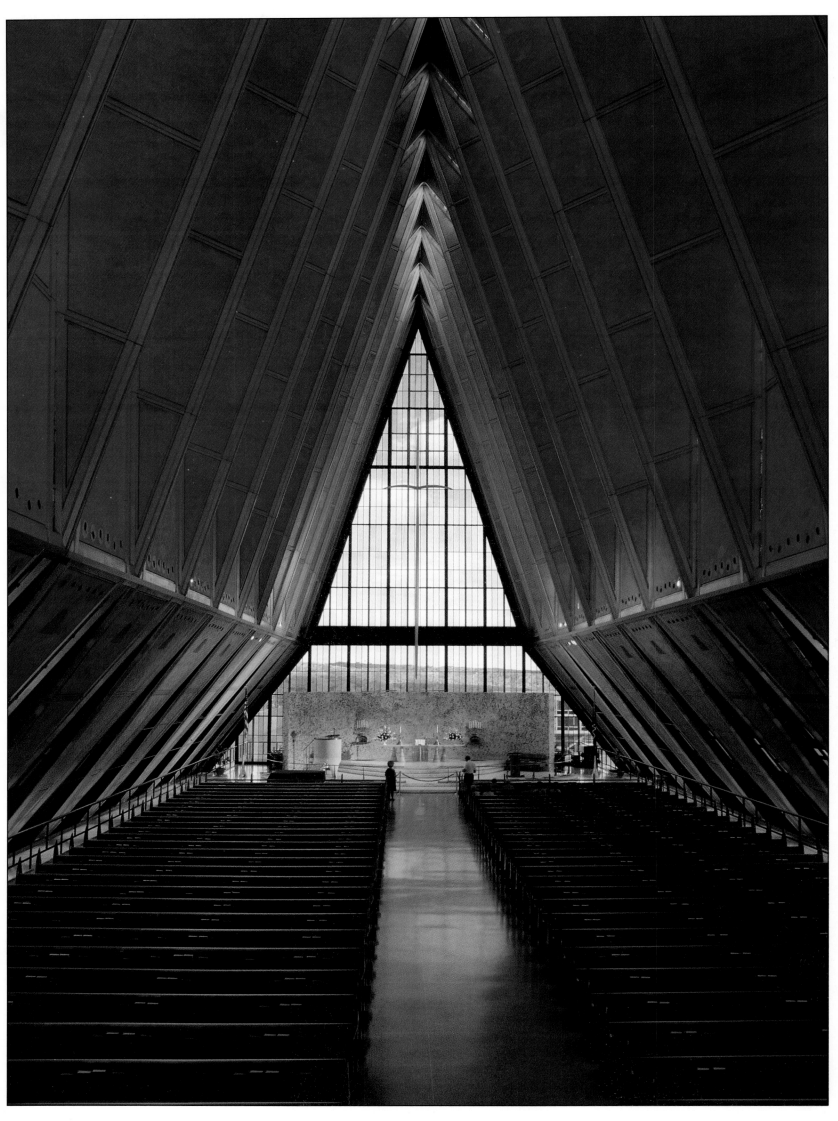

Above: light filters through stained glass in the Protestant Chapel, one of several chapels under the one roof of the Air Force Academy Cadet Chapel on the U.S. Air Force Academy base (facing page) at Colorado Springs. Designed to center attention on both the sky that the cadets, as pilots, are learning to master and upon Heaven, this chapel aspires to a harmonious blend of the physical and the spiritual worlds.

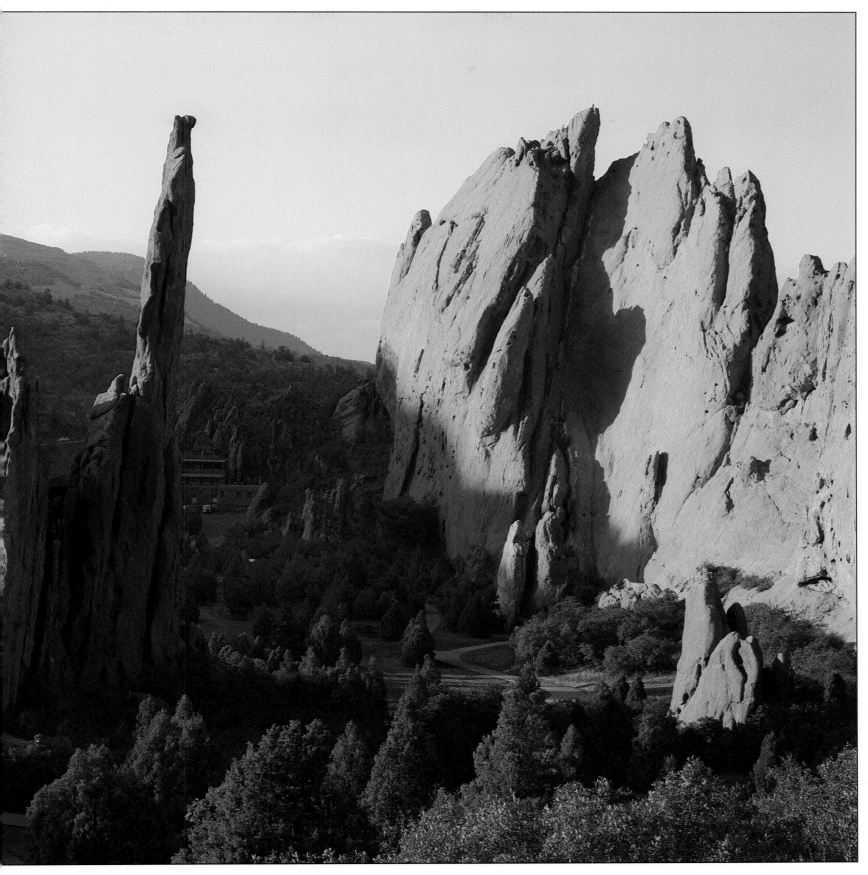

Above left: sturdy and apparently bewigged lions stand guard outside the pink granite Shrine of the Sun, a memorial to the cowboy comedian, Will Rogers, on Cheyenne Mountain near Colorado Springs. Also near this major resort, at Manitou Springs, lies the Garden of the Gods (left and above), a park containing an almost surreal group of red sandstone monoliths, reminiscent of Ayers Rock in the Australian outback.

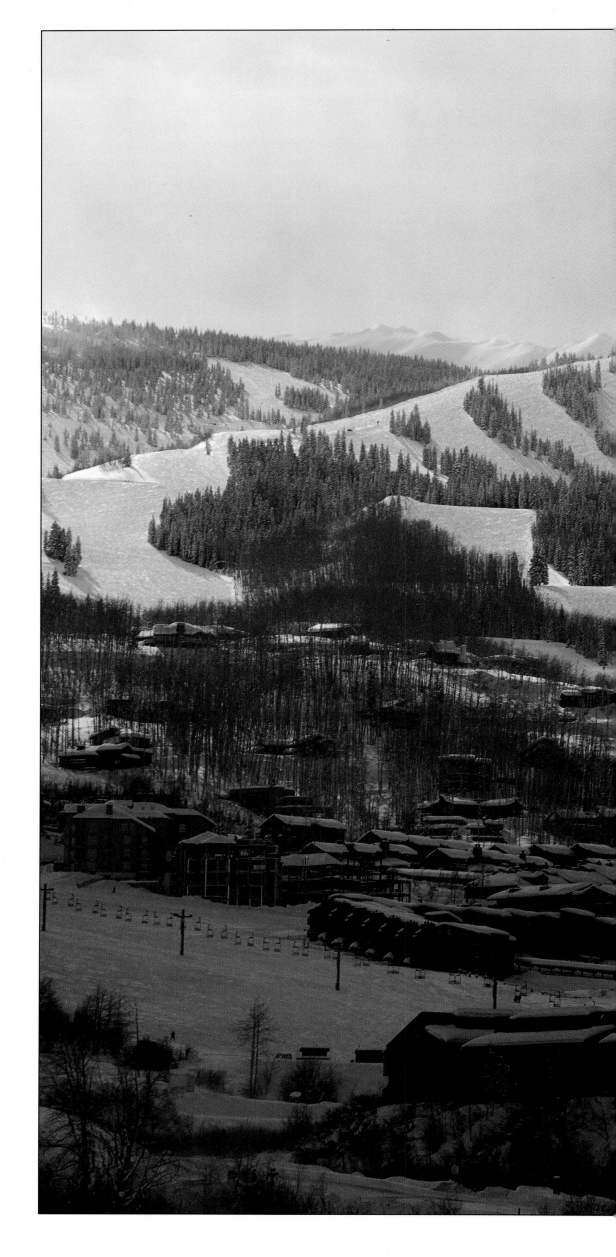

A light fall of the champagne powder snow for which Snowmass is famous ices the conifers on Snowmass Mountain. Snowmass Ski Area, ten miles from Aspen, is the third largest resort of its kind in North America – thirteen chairlifts serve over 1,500 acres of skiable terrain criss-crossed by fifty-five miles of trails. Essentially a family resort, Snowmass encourages children to join in with the fun by providing them with their own ski program – "Snowmass Snowbunnies" can be as young as three years old. For more advanced skiers, the resort offers a tempting array of imaginatively named slopes, such as Velvet Falls, Lunch Line Dawdler and the Big Burn. Overleaf: a winter's afternoon draws to a close in Vail.

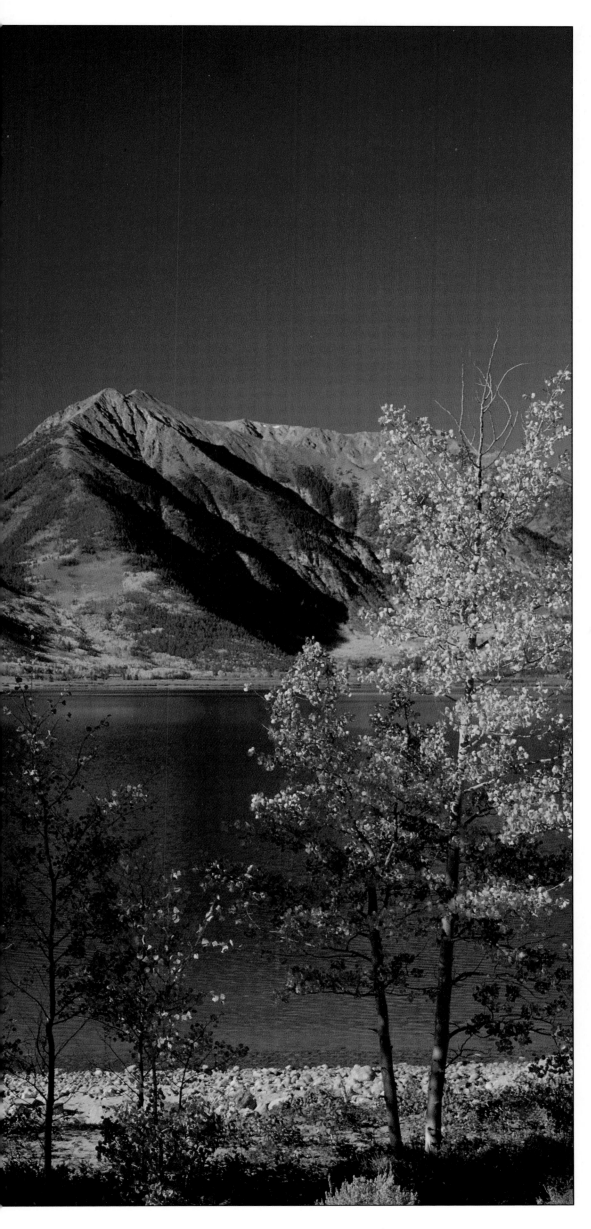

Aspens so bright they seem bedecked with gold pieces line the autumn shores of Twin Lakes Reservoir. This stretch of water is actually one lake whose name probably arose because of the extreme narrowing at its center – on a map this strip of water is so slender as to be overlooked at first glance. The reservoir lies close to both the highest mountain in the American Rockies, Mount Elbert, which rises to 14,433 feet, and to tortuous Independence Pass (overleaf), a mountain route that reaches a height of 12,000 feet to connect the ski-resort town of Aspen with Leadville.

Aspen (above) is perhaps Colorado's most famous ski resort, renowned for both the quality of its skiing and the glamour of its clientele – it has long been favored by film stars. Born of a silver rush in the 1880s – Victorian architecture (left) can still be seen in the town – a decade later Aspen was home to nearly 12,000 people. The good times did not last, however, and the town could claim only 600 inhabitants by the 'Thirties. After the Second World War, though, an infant ski industry swiftly came of age and each winter Aspen grew steadily more prosperous as a consequence of another kind of silver – snow.

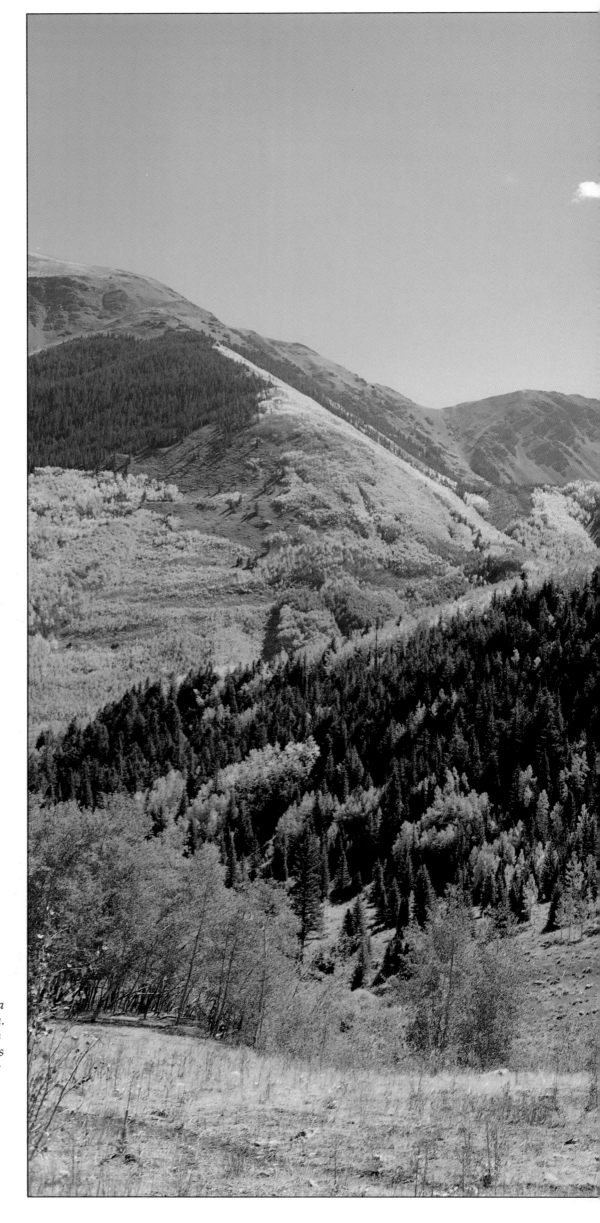

Fall rests lightly on the mountains around Ashcroft Ski Area, which lies south of Aspen in Gunnison National Forest. This protected reserve, which covers over a million acres, was named for one Captain Gunnison, an Indian-fighter and railroad surveyor who explored the region in 1853. Gunnison was murdered whilst trying to explain to the Indians that he was not a settler but an explorer – they did not believe him. The forest includes twenty-seven peaks in excess of 12,000 feet, is laced with trout-fishing streams and studded with high mountain lakes. Near the Ashcroft Ski Area lie the deserted cabins of Ashcroft, a ghost town since 1900.

Close to its source on the flanks of Castle Peak, Maroon Creek races (above) towards its confluence with the Roaring Fork River at Aspen, though further downstream (right) it flows at a more sober rate, past the debris cast onto its banks during the spring torrents, now bleached by a season of sunshine. Overleaf: the warmth of summer fails to rid the Maroon Bells – Aspen's most famous landmark – of their last pockets of snow, now soon to be replenished as fall approaches.

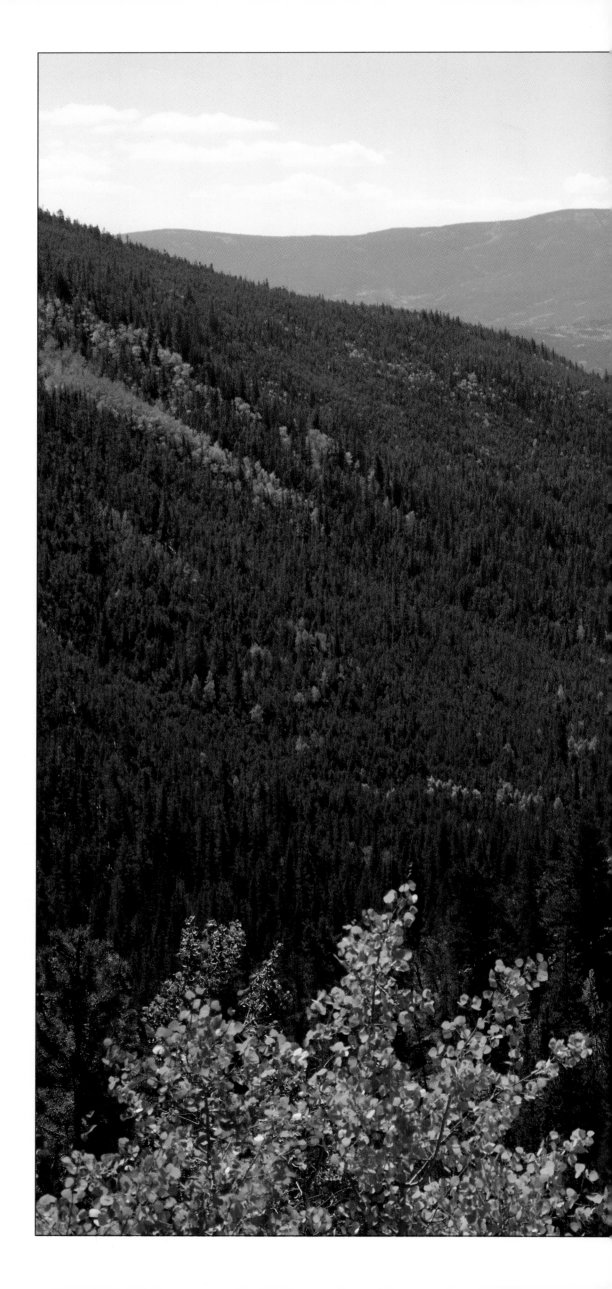

Embraced by San Isabel National Forest, a highway of hairpin bends finds a way through the Sawatch Range, the highest section of the southern Rocky Mountains. Two highways traverse these mountains, scaling Independence and Monarch passes, both of which exceed 11,000 feet. Such altitudes ensure that snowfall makes these routes impassable in winter – it is then that the 1.7-mile-long Eisenhower tunnel under the Rockies near Denver comes into its own.

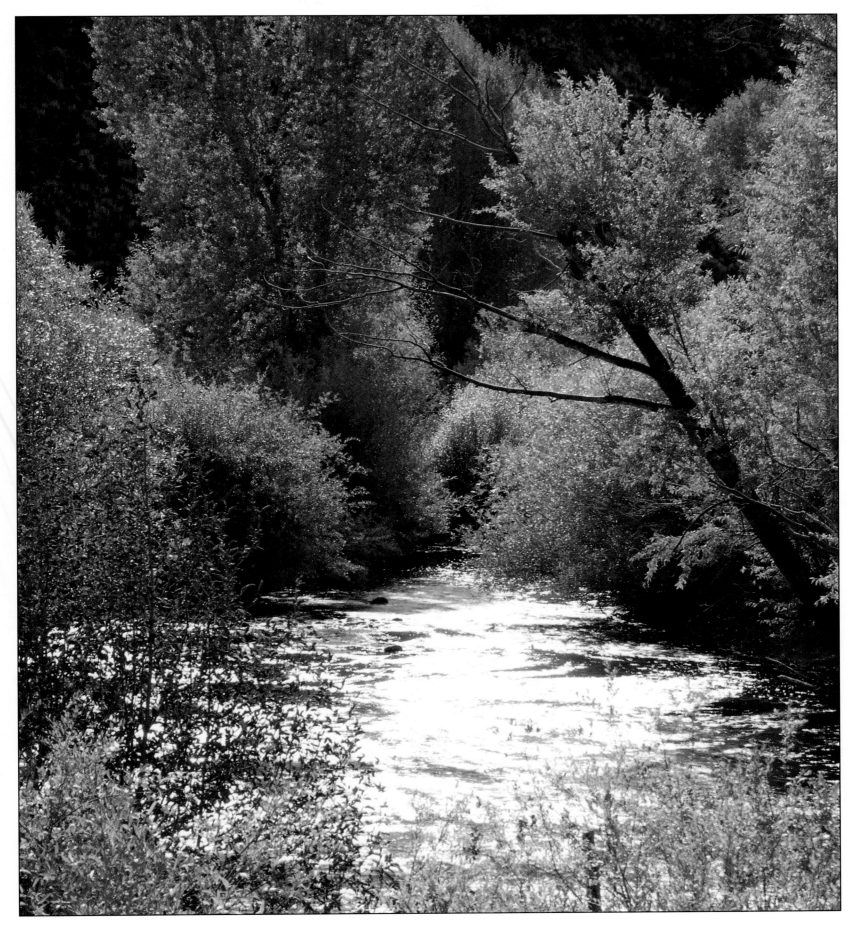

Facing page: cattle graze on sun-dried pasture near Doyleville in Gunnison County, seven miles from Quartz Creek (above) at Parlin, the next stop along State Highway 50 en route to Gunnison town. This county in southwest Colorado is famous for its fishing, and Quartz Creek is one of the region's renowned trout-fishing streams. Gunnison County can boast 1,300 miles of streams and lake shoreline, a fact that has made it the Mecca of Colorado anglers.

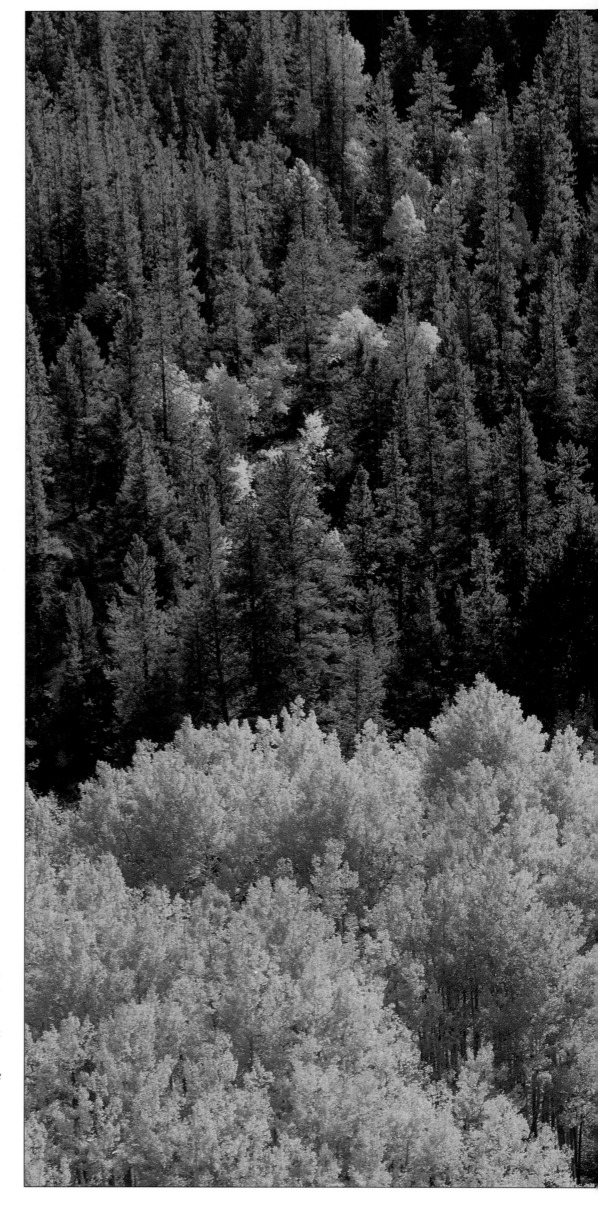

*Tomichi Creek, on its way to Blue Mesa
Reservoir in Gunnison National Forest,
southwest Colorado. This is the land of the black
bear, the elk and the mountain lion – not for
nothing is Colorado one of America's most
popular hunting regions, as all these animals are
on the list of big game that can be shot here, once
a license has been obtained for the purpose.
Unlike Colorado's national parks, where wildlife
is protected from the gun, its national forests can
be used for seasonal hunting. However, there are
restrictions upon the shooting of the state's
bighorn sheep and Rocky Mountain goats – these
can only be taken by Colorado residents.*

The white water, green algae and sandy rock of the Crystal River echo the colors of the mixed woodland on its banks. This river rises amid the mountains of Gunnison National Forest near now-deserted Marble, a Colorado mining town with a difference. Here, instead of precious metals, a precious stone – marble – was the prize; a few miles from the town lies a huge cavern in the side of a mountain from which the marble was taken for Lincoln's Memorial and the Tomb of the Unknown Soldier in Washington D.C. Such was the demand that Marble's community was once 2,000 people strong, but today only a few empty log cabins remain.

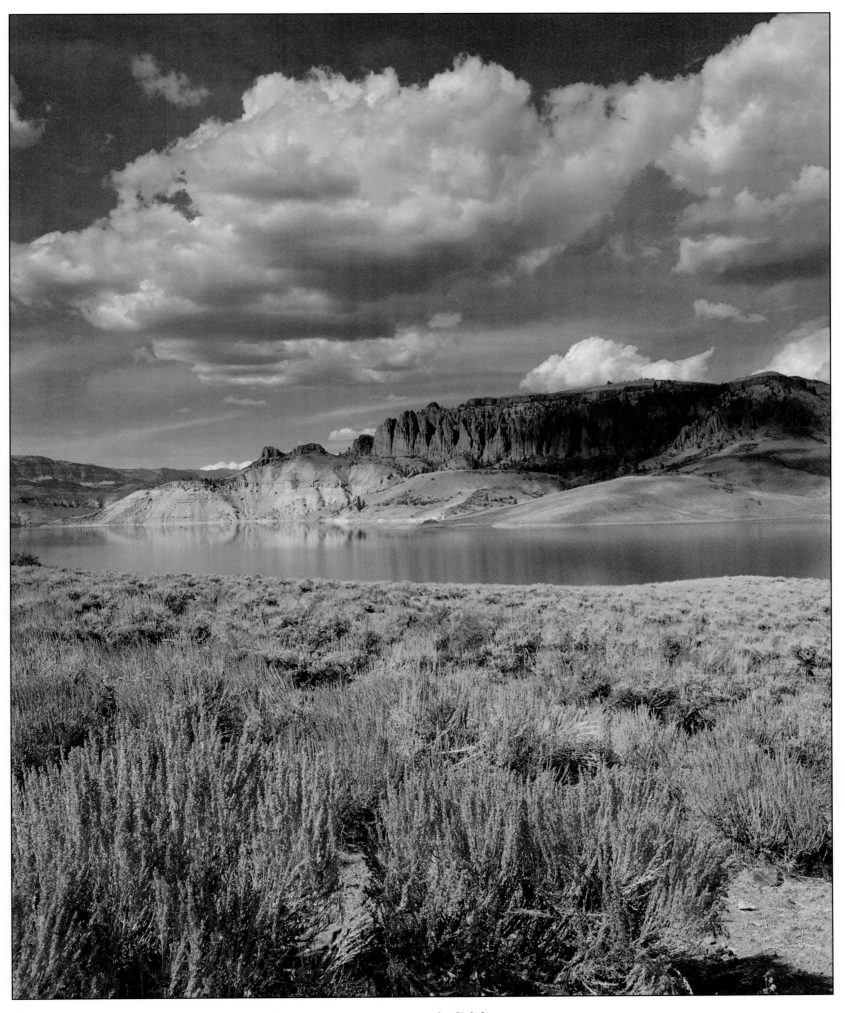

Facing page: the stark, serrated edges of the Gunnison River's Black Canyon, only slightly softened by its fringe of tenacious conifers. This awe-inspiring, two-million-year-old canyon is fittingly named, being so narrow and deep that little sunlight penetrates down to the river some two thousand feet below. Descent into the canyon is considered unwise throughout the year, and is virtual suicide in winter. Above: serene Blue Mesa Reservoir, which lies east of Montrose, and is drained by the Gunnison River.

Yellowing aspens signal summer's end beside the Cimarron River (left) and along the banks of the Crystal River (overleaf). The former river rises in Uncompahgre National Forest, the latter in Gunnison National Forest, and both waterways are tributaries of the Gunnison River, which drains much of southwest Colorado. Rivers of national importance, such as the magnificent Colorado, Missouri and Rio Grande, rise in the Rockies, their waters comprising largely of snowmelt as here snow forms a greater proportion of the annual precipitation than rain. In fact, these mountains are quite arid – during the last century, many ill-equipped fortune hunters died of thirst while trying to cross them. These days, wherever feasible, reservoirs have been constructed to conserve precious water supplies.

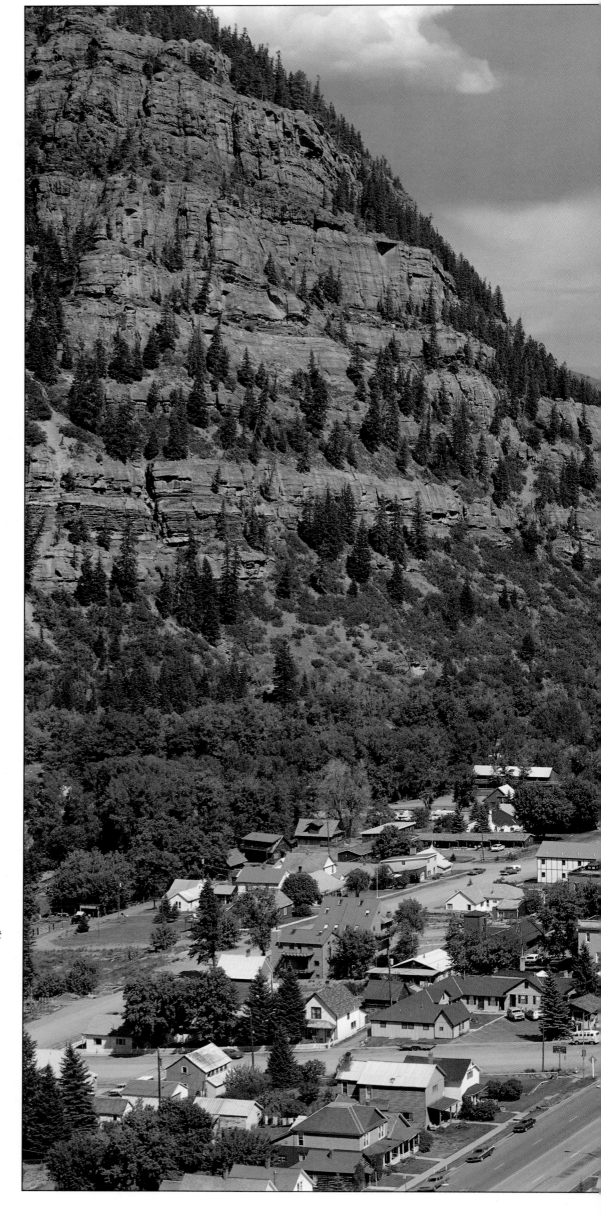

The small mountain community of Ouray, a mining town which lies some seven thousand feet above sea level in the heart of Uncompahgre National Forest and is named after a chief of the fierce Ute Indian tribes. The surrounding mountains are considered to be some of the loveliest in the Rockies. Ouray can boast several hot springs and a number of buildings of historical interest, including – rather grandly – an opera hall. It is reached along U.S. Highway 550, a route nicknamed the "Million Dollar Highway" after it was discovered that it had been unknowingly paved with low-grade ores.

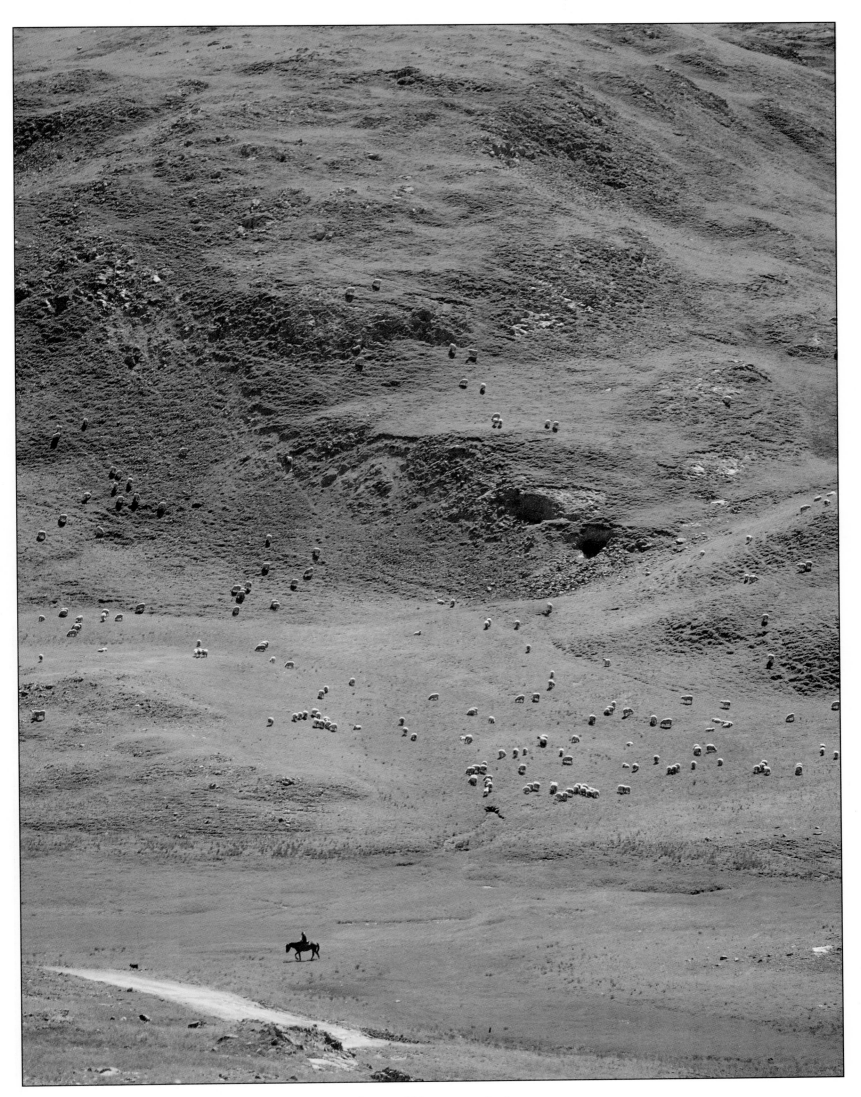

Facing page: jeep trails in Uncompahgre National Forest near Ouray, which are recognized as being some of the best in the state. The scenery around this town is imposing, a number of the mountains being "fourteeners" – Rocky Mountain parlance for a peak over 14,000 feet high. Many of the trails are above the timberline, and may run through breathtaking mountain passes, sometimes leading to ghost towns or disused mines. Above: a lone "sheepboy" tends some of the state's one million sheep on pasture in the Western Rockies.

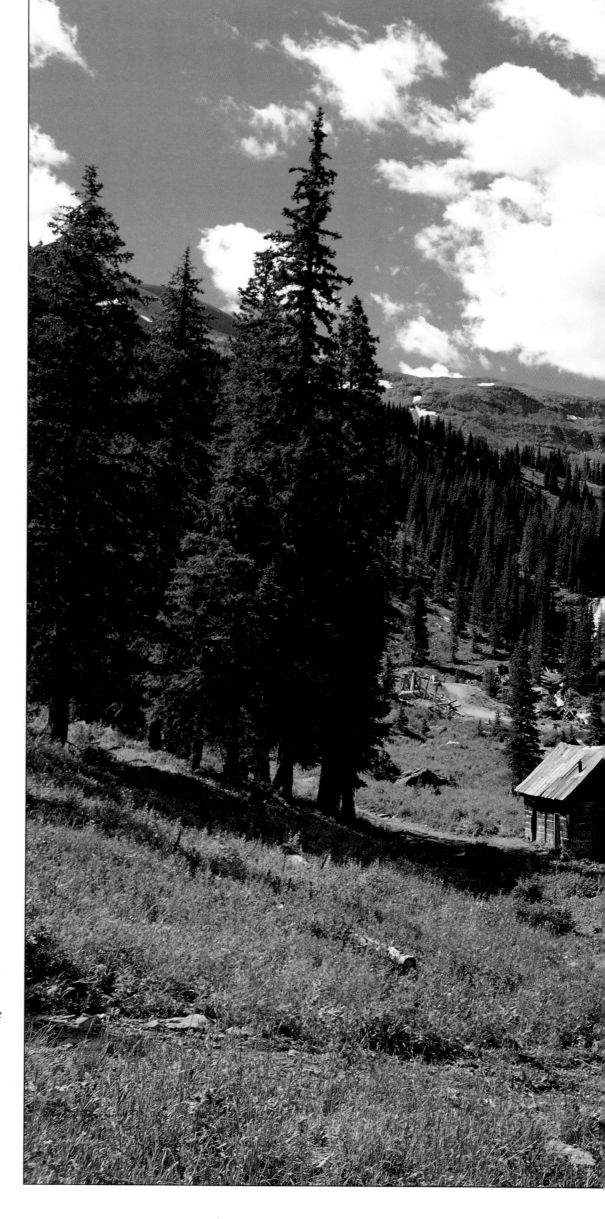

A modest log cabin practically sited near a stream on Engineer Pass, close to Engineer Mountain, an impressive peak of some 12,900 feet in the La Plata Range of San Juan National Forest. Throughout the Rockies, from the windows of remote cabins such as this, nineteenth-century trappers could have expected to see a wide variety of animals and birds, including the American peregrine falcon and the bald eagle, the nation's national bird, which were then quite common sights. The situation has changed, however, and today these birds are on the endangered species list – San Juan National Forest is one of the few places left in the Rockies where they may still be seen.

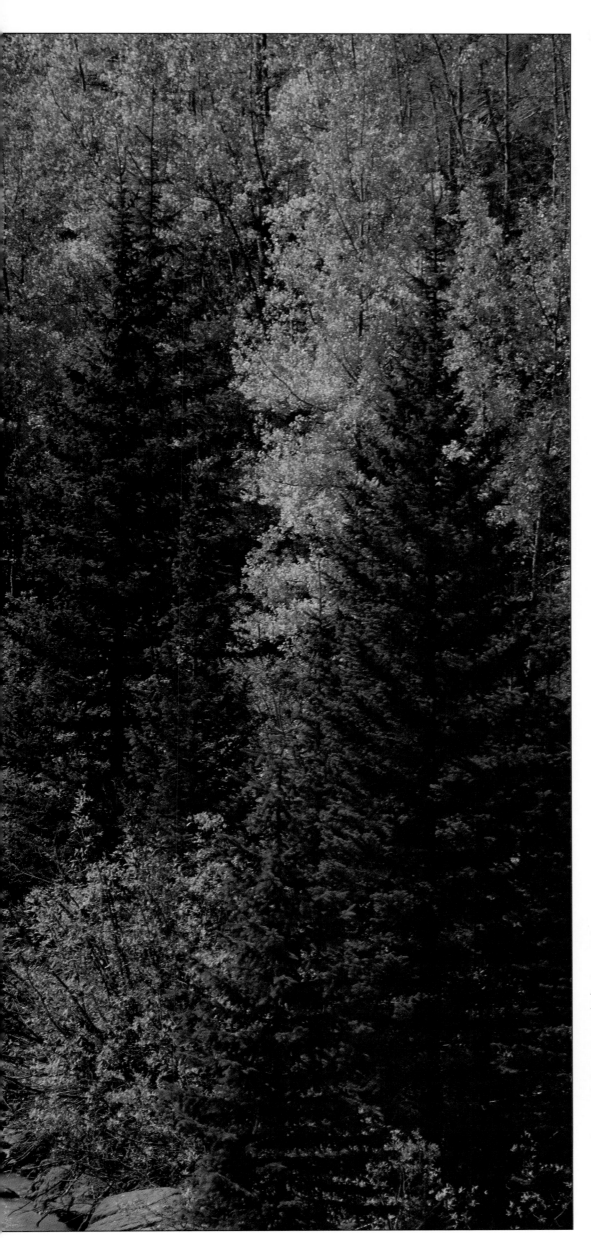

No bigger than a stream and as rusty gold as the deciduous trees upon its banks, the Uncompahgre River rises in Uncompahgre National Forest to start its hundred-mile-long journey to join the Gunnison River at Delta, from there to mingle ultimately with the great Colorado – another river distinctively reddish in color. Not only are the rivers colorful in this national forest, the mountains are too. The Uncompahgre's source is close to the Red Mountains, several peaks conspicuous from Highway 550 south of Ouray. Their reddish hue makes them easily discernible by day, and when the sun sets they can appear as vivid as glowing coals.

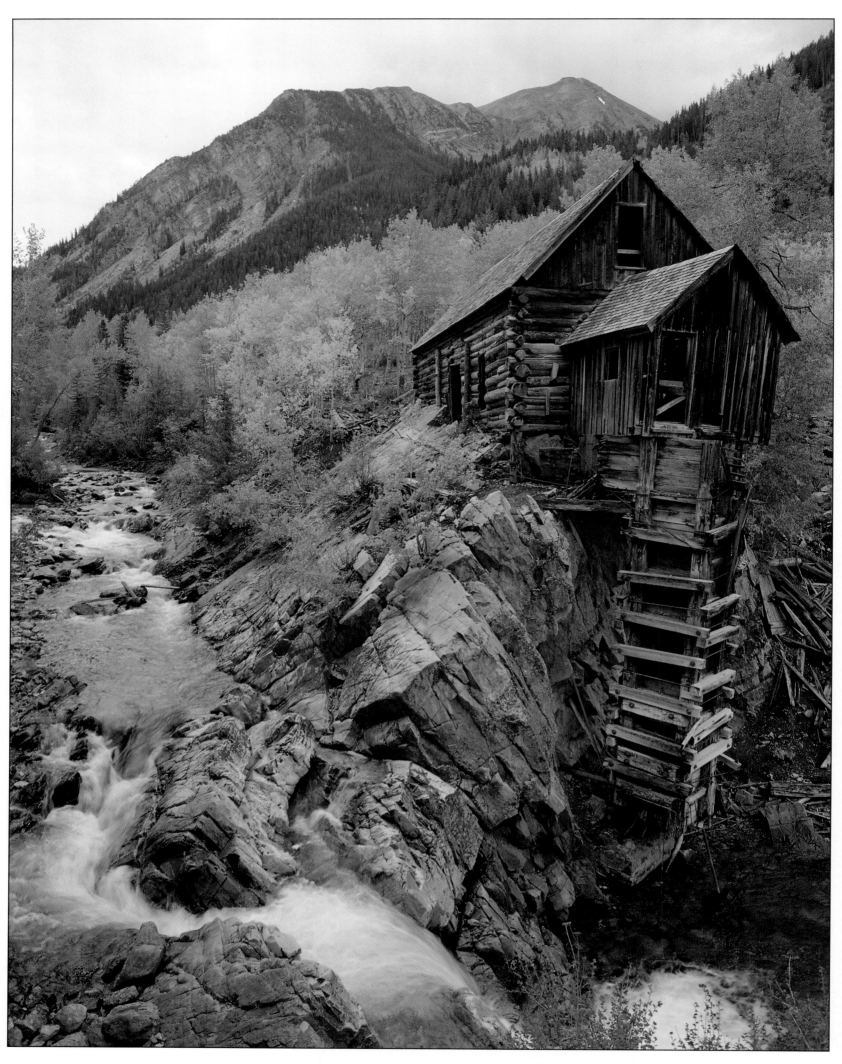

Above: precariously perched, Deadhorse Mill clings to the bank of the Crystal River. The mill is a relic from the nineteenth century, when it served nearby Crystal City, then a mining town.
Facing page: the ghost town of Sneffels, the spoil heap in the background evidence of the proximity of the mines that gave rise to the town during the last century. As recently as the 'Forties, such towns could be found with plates still on the tables and bottles on the saloon shelves, but a renewed interest in ghost towns since has meant that all such artefacts have been removed by sightseers.

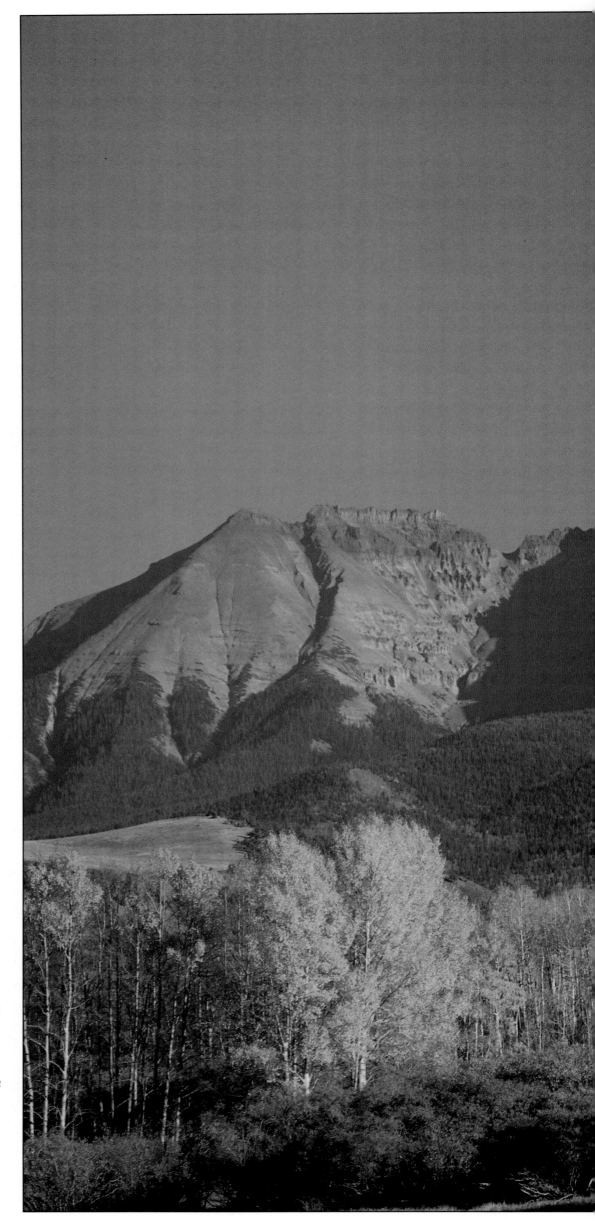

The Sneffels Range in southwest Colorado,
dominated by Mount Sneffels (overleaf), which
rises to the impressive height of 14,150 feet.
Usually dull gray above the treeline, these
mountains seem to change color completely in
the light of the setting sun. On such exposed and
rocky slopes as these Rocky Mountain goats,
exceptionally good climbers, may still be found.
In the summer, their white, woolly coat –
excellent camouflage in the winter – makes them
easy to spot, but their surefootedness allows them
to take advantage of every foothold in escaping
the unwelcome attention of man.

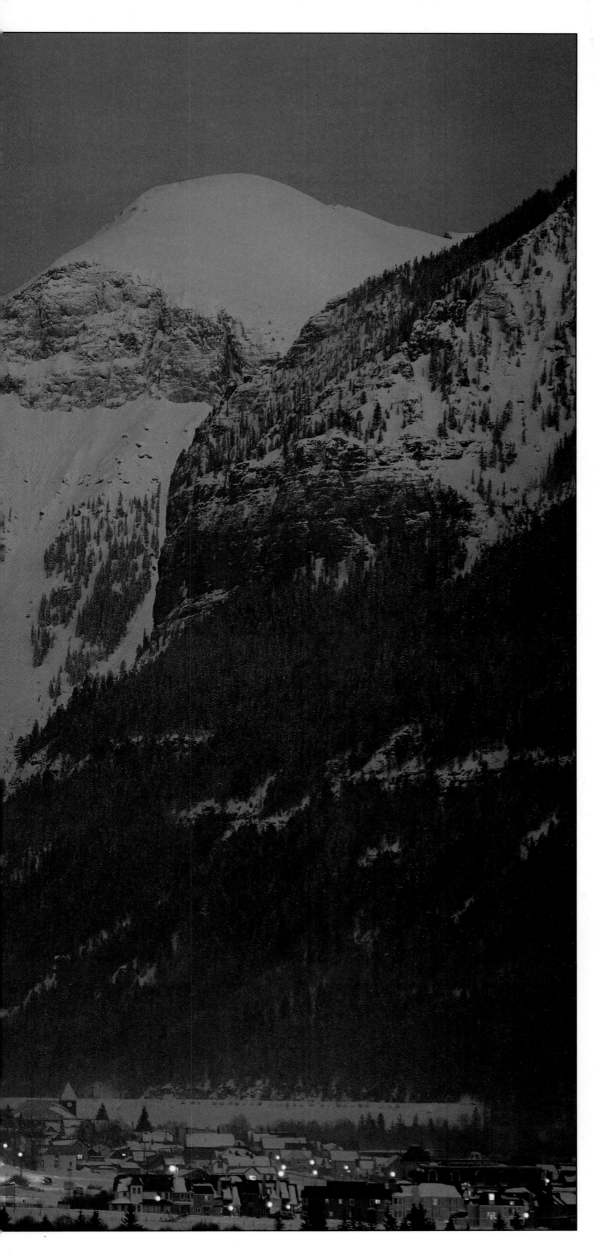

Telluride twinkles in the dusk at the end of a box canyon in the San Juan Mountains. Viewed like this, tucked up in snow at night, it is easy to appreciate why this charming old town is a national historical landmark. Though it is one of Colorado's numerous ski resorts, due to its remote situation and its size Telluride remains uncrowded and old-fashioned, a small community with just one main street boasting a variety of well-preserved Victorian facades (overleaf). Interestingly, though, in the nineteenth century its remote situation didn't save Telluride's bank from being robbed by Butch Cassidy ....

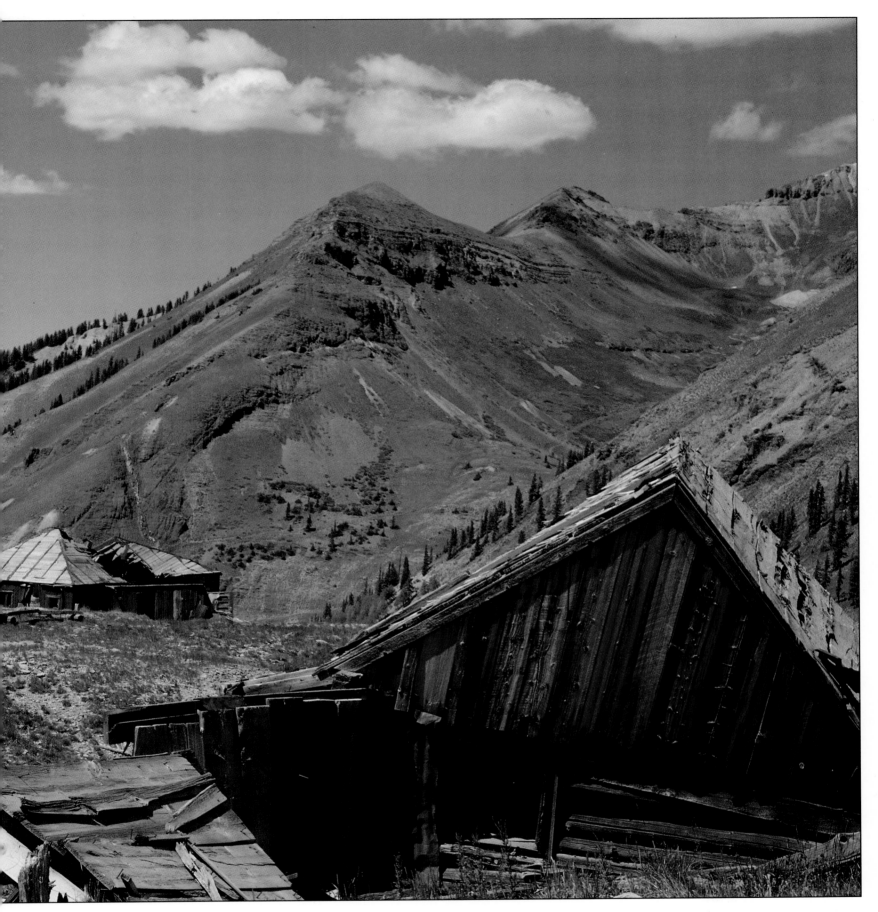

Above left: collapsing roof planks fan out above a cabin entrance in Alta, a ghost town which lies south of Telluride. Also close to Telluride lies Tomboy (left and above), another mining town whose tumbledown remains are extensive, but the road to Tomboy has been described as "a throat-clutching cliff-hanger," so reaching the site can require almost as much courage as that demanded of the miners who braved this mountain a century ago.

Stiff, sharply pointed conifers find a foothold on seemingly impenetrable rocky outcrops in Imogen Pass in the San Juan Mountains near Telluride. After their formation, with the rest of the Rockies, by the collision of two continental plates, the San Juan Mountains were further shaped by volcanic activity, today forming a sometimes bleak and always challenging landscape for the hiker and the mountaineer.

A Black Bear Pass jeep trail known as Tomboy Road zigzags down a steep mountainside between Telluride and Ouray in the San Juan Mountains. Only four-wheel drive vehicles are suitable for such terrain, and many such routes in these mountains are described as "white knuckle" rides, even when driven in a jeep. Nevertheless, aficionados flock to the San Juans to drive these trails as they are considered to be some of the most exhilarating in the country. Overleaf: fireweed flourishes beside Alta Lake in the San Juan Mountains.

Above: Silverton, whose name is supposedly derived from a miner's boast "We might not have much else, but we've got a ton of silver," is a former mining town that lies some nine thousand feet above sea level in the San Juan Mountains. Some of the town's Victorian buildings have been preserved and reminders of the past (above left) are to be found everywhere, particularly along Silverton's narrow guage railway (left).

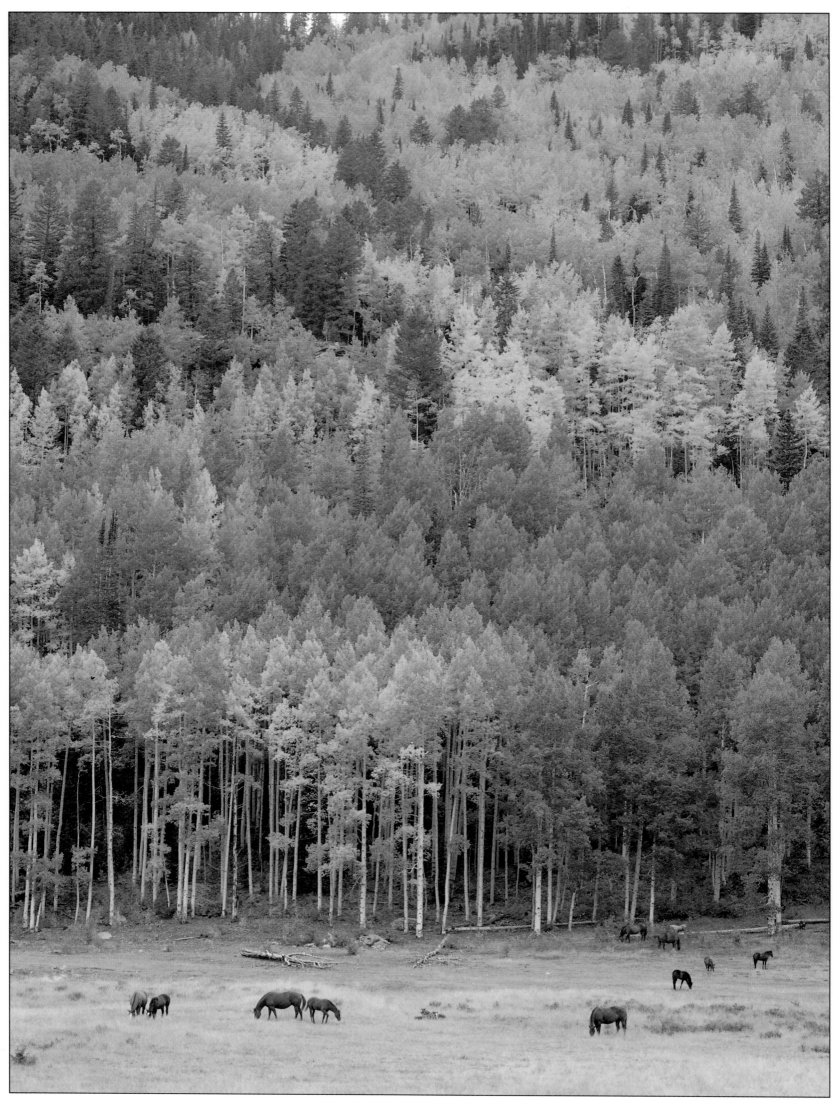

Above: a fine herd of mares and foals grazes companionably in a mountain pasture in southwest Colorado – even today, horseback riding remains one of the finest ways of seeing the Rockies. Facing page: beyond a foreground of silhouetted conifers, the Red Mountains seem to burn in the light of the rising sun. Set in the midst of the San Juan range these peaks guard a pass between Telluride and Silverton that stands over eleven thousand feet above sea level.

Above left: Trout Lake, a small alpine fishing lake that lies close to Lizard Head Pass in Uncompahgre National Forest. Above: a scoured cliff cradles the narrow, shallow infant Rio Grande just south of Creede, while twenty miles downstream, outside the town of South Forks, the river (left) noticeably widens on its 1,885-mile journey to the Gulf of Mexico. During the Civil War the Confederates sailed up the Rio Grande in a bid to seize the Colorado goldfields, but were forced to retreat in 1862.

Lowering clouds hang in empty threat over the soft golds of rabbitbrush and prairie grass that blanket the San Luis Valley in the extreme south of the state. This alpine valley is a desert the size of Puerto Rico, inhospitable to both man and beast and consequently one of the state's least populated areas. Yet what the region lacks in agricultural wealth is more than compensated for by its geological significance. The desert's highlight is Great Sand Dunes National Monument (overleaf), a collection of peaks formed over thousands of years as sand has been blown the length of the desert and trapped at the foot of the Sangre de Christo mountain range.

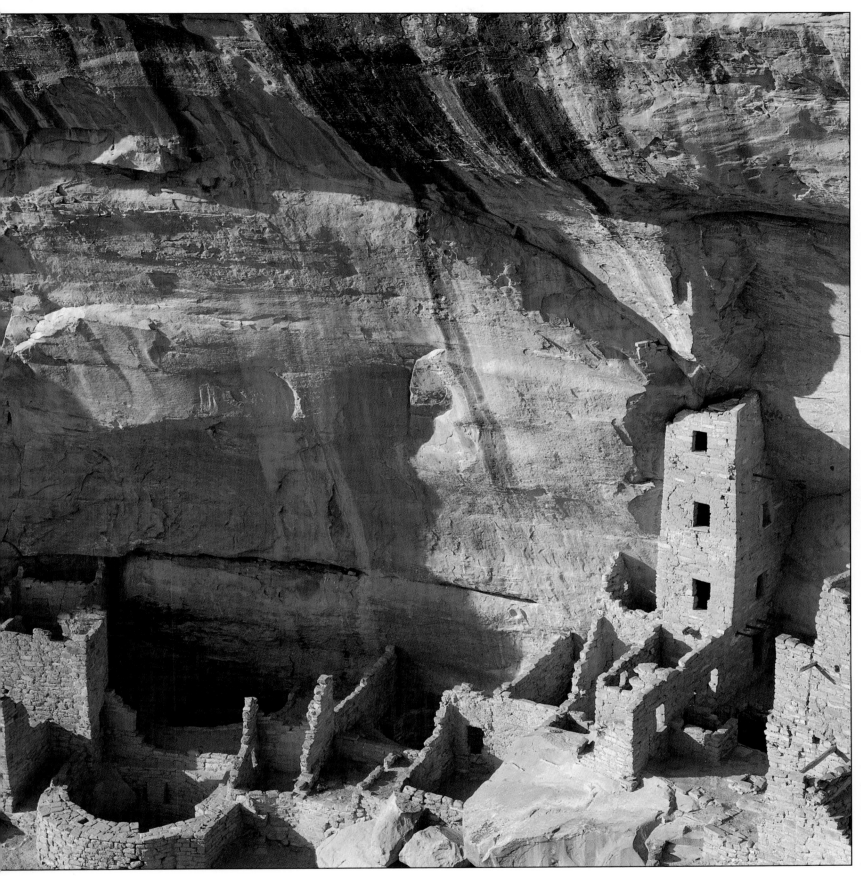

These pages: Mesa Verde National Park, a nationally famous site in southwest Colorado set aside to preserve more than 350 groups of Indian cliff dwellings (left and above) of considerable archaeological importance. Pueblo Indians lived here from the time of Christ until the end of the thirteenth century; pottery, woven fabrics and decorated walls – all of great artistic worth – were found here a mere hundred years ago. Little had changed since the Indians had left as the area was thought to be haunted and local tribes had not ventured into the ruins to find out for certain. Overleaf: Cliff Palace, the finest of these dwellings, and (following page) a Colorado sundown.

INDEX